When the Fighting is Over

TUMBLEDOWN

When the Fighting is Over

TUMBLEDOWN

A Personal Story

JOHN LAWRENCE
and ROBERT LAWRENCE MC
with Carol Price

BLOOMSBURY

First published in Great Britain 1988
Copyright © 1988 by John Lawrence and Robert Lawrence MC
This paperback edition published in 1988

Bloomsbury Publishing Ltd, 2 Soho Square, London W1V 5DE

British Library Cataloguing in Publication Data

Lawrence, John
    When the fighting is over: a personal story of the
    battle for Tumbledown mountain and its aftermath.
    1. Falkland Islands War. Personal observations.
    I. Title II. Lawrence, Robert
    997′.11

    ISBN 0-7475-0288-9

Printed in Great Britain by Richard Clay Ltd
Bungay, Suffolk

ACKNOWLEDGEMENTS

I am most grateful for the encouragement that Charles Wood gave me when I first thought of writing this book and, although it is not the book of his film 'Tumbledown', I derived much inspiration from his brilliant script. My thanks are also due to my dear wife Jean, the rest of my family and our many friends, without whose support I could not have come through the five and a half years since Robert was shot.

To Ian Robertson I owe a great deal. His advice, help and friendship have been very reassuring.

The idea of incorporating Robert's first-hand story into mine was that of Nigel Newton and David Reynolds. It is undoubtedly a better book for that contribution and we must thank Carol Price for her help with the preparation of that part of the manuscript.

JOHN LAWRENCE

* * *

I would like to thank those people who were involved in developing the film *Tumbledown* precursor to this book: Mark Burns, Charles Wood and Alan Wright in the beginning, and Richard Broke and Richard Eyre who brought it to an outstanding conclusion.

ROBERT LAWRENCE

'I will go, I will go
When the fighting is over
To the land of Macleod
That I left to be a soldier
I will go, I will go.'

PICTURE CREDITS

Ken Kelly, page 2 *right*
Paul Haley/*Soldier* magazine, page 3 *bottom* and page 6 *bottom*
London Evening Standard, page 8 *top*
Adrienne Overall, page 8 *bottom left*
Lieutenant-Colonel P. Roberts, page 4 and page 5 *top and bottom*
Tom Smith/*Daily Express*, page 7 *top*
Western Telegraph, page 7 *bottom*

CONTENTS

INTRODUCTION

John Lawrence

The chill November wind ruffled Robert's long fair hair as he stood before the tall grey stone cross. His left hand, heavy and with no feeling at the end of his paralysed arm, was thrust deep in the trouser pocket of his smart double-breasted blue serge suit. It was always a struggle stuffing it in there from the wrong side with his good right hand, but once there it was out of the way, and the deep side vent in the jacket allowed it to be covered in such a way as to make it look casual and relaxed. Almost matching his hair, the yellow silk lining of his suit flashed and his boots, worn to support his spastic left ankle, gleamed through the long grass of the churchyard just as they had done when he commanded the Queen's Guard at the Tower of London three years and seven months before. On his breast the Military Cross, the General Service Medal with Northern Ireland clasp and the South Atlantic Star with Falkland Islands rosette blazed their colours proudly.

The congregation had dispersed, and Robert stood there alone, staring at the wreath of poppies that his mother, churchwarden of St Mary's, Barnes, had placed at the foot of the war memorial. Then his gaze dropped to the small wooden cross with the single poppy in the centre, which had been stuck in the grass beside the memorial when no one had been about earlier that morning. On it was written:

W.O. II D Wight, Gdsman Tanbini,
Gdsman Reynolds, D.C.M.
and 5 Others of 2 Bn Scots Guards

INTRODUCTION

Tumbledown Mountain, 14th June 1982
'Nemo me impune lacessit'

The irony of that royal motto, 'No one wounds me with impunity', hit hard, though not as hard as the 7.62 high-velocity armour-piercing bullet that had passed through his head in that ferocious battle, destroying about forty-five per cent of his brain.

Robert brushed a tear from his eye and walked to the low churchyard wall, his limp marked and awkward as he picked his way round the old gravestones. After a few minutes alone with his thoughts he turned and, smiling wanly, rejoined us on the path to the lych-gate which was itself a memorial to those who had fallen in the Boer War. The words of the intercession that morning came back.

'We pray for all those who have fought for their country through the centuries, remembering especially those from this parish such as Colonel Morley of the 79th Highlanders and Private Wood of the East Surreys, whose names are the first and last on the wall of the lych-gate. We ask forgiveness for the waste of human life sacrificed so often to achieve a better world, yet dissipated by the greed and stupidity of those who follow afterwards. But also, oh Lord, we give thanks for the courage and the bravery, the love and compassion, the comradeship, the tenderness and the pure selflessness and chivalry that has so often shone through the darkness of wars. Help us never to despise these human virtues implanted in us by you.

'We remember all those wounded in war. Grant to them strength and courage, hope and cheerfulness. Comfort all those who still know the fear of conflict. Take from their minds the horrors of the mud and barbed wire of Flanders, the barrage of guns at El Alamein or Casino, the stench of the jungles of Kohima, the deprivation of prison camps, the scream of Stukas or the thud of depth charges — the smell of burning on the *Sir Galahad*, the freezing crags of Tumbledown Mountain.'

A FORCES FAMILY

John Lawrence

'You haven't got time for gardening, Daddy — not even in a thirty-by-forty plot like this. What you need is a lot of hard surface work, paving, gravel, a few raised brick beds, a pond perhaps and a fountain with shrubs and New Zealand flax and bamboo, lots of ground cover and creepers on the walls.'

For all that my three sons are grown men, it gives me quite a thrill, secretly, when they call me 'Daddy'. This was Nick, the second and the biggest of the three. He's also the gentlest, in a way, though he's had his moments on the rugby field. Very intelligent, but dyslexic, his academic achievement was poor and so he had turned to the land, back to Mother Earth as it were. After a year at the Royal Agricultural College, Cirencester, and three on a dairy farm, he now has his own successful landscape gardening firm. As always, he was being the commonsensical one, the pragmatic, thoroughly logical one. 'In three years' time, say 1982, this garden will look lovely and no work for you to keep it so' was his final seal on the conversation. Well, he had done the Lord Mayor's garden and the one in St James's Square, so why not mine.

The faded Union flag fluttered proudly on its pole thrust into the corner bed above the pond, just in front of the bamboo. It had been Grandma's and had flown on every Coronation Day, royal wedding or British victory since 1918. From the conservatory, Christopher, Nick's elder brother, emerged with glasses and a bottle of sparkling something or other. He literally danced around the New Zealand flax as he sang, 'Who do you think you are kidding, Galtieri?' We all laughed nervously, big Nick and his lovely wife Melanie, my wife Jean and I, and Robert — Lieutenant Robert Alasdair Davidson Lawrence, Scots Guards. It hardly seemed possible that we were gathering to say goodbye to the baby of the family, who was going off to war eight thousand miles away.

I could not get out of my mind two pictures, one of my father driving off from school leaving me waving on the grass as he left for Burma in 1942, and the other, much more vivid, of myself leaning from the window of the train as it pulled out of Wendover station to take me on my way to serve Her Majesty in Egypt, leaving Jean in tears and heavily pregnant with Chris, her WRAF officer's raincoat barely reaching round her. She was so lovely and so brave.

When Robert finally went, he embraced us each in turn and there were tears in all our eyes. As I held him to me, the grip of his hand like iron, I said quietly, 'I know you'll do well, but be careful and keep your head down.'

'I will, Daddy, I will.'

There were still two days before the battalion would set sail on the QE2, but we did not see Robert again before he left. We had not expected to, but Chris saw him, of course.

Chris had always been very much big brother to the other two, and he too had served in the Scots Guards. His advice would be invaluable and in any case he would expect to give it.

One Thursday evening towards the end of his last term at school, Christopher had slipped out and phoned from an Edinburgh call box. 'Look, Daddy, I want to try this new limited short-service commission in the Army between now and going up to Cambridge but the Major in the Corps says I'm too young. I have to be eighteen by 6 February and I'm not eighteen until 12 March. Can you please speak to someone?'

Good old Daddy fix-it, I thought, but of course on the Friday morning I rang the number in the Army advertisements and asked for the poor chap whose name was in the advert, Major Bob Gurdon.

'I'm awfully sorry, your son is too young and the applications had to be in by last Monday.'

'Oh,' I said, 'you mean he's five weeks too young and five days too late.'

'That's about the size of it, I'm afraid.'

'Tell me, how many places have you got?'

'Thirty.'

'And how many applicants?'

'Fifty-nine.'

'Good gracious,' I said, 'give Christopher a chance and you'll have a choice of one in two.'

'Well, there just isn't time, there's medicals to arrange and all the paperwork.'

'All right, let's put it another way. What you are saying is that a 1st XV coloursman and school prefect at Fettes, a corporal in the Corps, with an "A" level A grade in History, B grade in English, C grade in French and a place at Cambridge already is the sort of boy that the British Army can afford to pass up!'

'Oh, well, Wing Commander, if you put it like that, maybe we can do something. It's still going to be difficult though, because we have to find a regiment that will take him and not all of them are very keen on this new scheme.'

'The Queen's Own Highlanders will take him,' I said.

'How do you know that?'

'Because I was serving in Sharjah with the RAF when they were also there and I remember discussing the scheme with Andrew Duncan, their CO, when it was first mooted in a letter to *The Times*. We both thought it a good idea and he said to me, "For instance, John, if your boy were interested I'd take him." I'm quite prepared to keep him to that.'

'You know Andrew Duncan?' said the much relieved Major Gurdon. 'How absolutely splendid. As a matter of fact we haven't got a Highlander for the scheme yet. I'm in the Black Watch myself!'

Christopher was one of only twenty-one accepted for the first course. I always thought it good that they had not dropped their standards to fill the other nine places. The Queen's Own Highlanders were very good to him, but at the end of university he transferred to the Scots Guards. Fort George and the Perth Hunt Ball did not really appeal to him. Fortunately the 1st Battalion Scots Guards had followed the Queen's Own Highlanders in Sharjah and again I had known the Commanding Officer. The introduction was useful, but of course it was Christopher who in the interview with the Lieutenant Colonel Commanding persuaded him to accept him in the regiment. This was no minor achievement with the fearsome Sir Gregor Macgregor of Macgregor!

Chris commanded his passing-out parade at Victory College, Sandhurst and after serving in Germany he went on Operation Drake in charge of the jungle survival section. This involved taking half a dozen youngsters into the Panamanian jungle for six days at a time, living off snakes, rats, parrots and insects. At the age of twenty-six he was Adjutant of the 1st Battalion Scots Guards, but after a year decided to leave. This in spite of protestations that he was destined to be a general. 'I don't want to be a general,' he had said, 'I want to make some money!' Three months later he was a trainee stockbroker and a trooper in the Artists Rifles, blacking his face every weekend and leaping out of aeroplanes. I was bound to tell him that going up in them in the first place was bad enough, but jumping out again was the height of stupidity.

In his turn Robert too had telephoned from Fettes to say he wanted to join the Army. It came as a complete surprise to me even though I had a photograph on my desk of him at the age of ten wearing his kilt and a beret, with a London Scottish swagger cane under his arm, saluting immaculately. It always made me laugh and I used to say to the photo, 'Get that smile off your face, soldier!'

He had five 'O' levels, was also a bit dyslexic though not as bad as Nick, and now reckoned he'd had enough of school. If he could come home he would go to a 'crammer', get his maths and then enter the Scots Guards the tough way, through Brigade Squad. I knew there was little point in trying to dissuade him once he had made up his mind.

Two days before the maths exam, Robert got mumps. He nevertheless insisted on going into town to take the exam. By the time he got there he was swollen on both sides, had a raging temperature and was sent home. He got over it, worked through Christmas and took his maths with another board in January. For the first time since getting his Duke of Edinburgh's Gold Award he had set his mind on achieving something. He got a 'B' grade pass and was accepted at Brigade Squad. At the Commissioning Selection Board which followed, his bizarre spelling almost floored him, but the system, pioneered largely through RAF aircrew selection, is the best in the world, and for once bureaucratic regulations did not come into it and Robert's innate leadership qualities were identified strongly enough to let him through to Sandhurst. Northern Ireland, Kenya and the Jungle Warfare Instructors' Course in Brunei followed, interspersed with the inevitable public duties.

At the Queen's Birthday Parade in 1981, as the programme proclaimed, Second Lieutenant Robert Lawrence, Scots Guards, was commanding No. 8 Guard, the first to march on to Horse Guards Parade. For me, as I watched with Jean from the stand, his word of command was immaculate and could be heard, I reckoned, in Putney. When he fell out and marched to the side of the parade ground, I thought I would burst with paternal pride. I had watched my father on parade at Plymouth Hoe for the King and Queen's Silver Jubilee in 1935. I had seen pictures of him commanding the Victory Parade in Bombay in 1945. As a Cranwell cadet I had loved the weekly commandant's parades and remembered slow-marching up the steps at my own commissioning parade taken by Admiral of the Fleet Lord Fraser of North Cape. I had seen Christopher command his own passing-out parade at Sandhurst, and now I was seeing Robert. Even though he was only commanding No. 8 Guard, I saw no one and nothing else on that parade apart from Her Majesty and the Pipes and Drums!

After Northern Ireland and Brunei, public duties soon began to pall and Robert became bored and restless. I worried that he was impatient and never content with his lot. He told me he had applied for intelligence duties in Northern Ireland and I almost scoffed at the idea. I just could not see that an 'up and at 'em' twenty-one-year-old could possibly be suitable for undercover work. I was shattered when he told me he had been selected. We did not tell his mother; well, not yet.

Jean and I took an old friend, Julia Farwell, to see the Ceremony of the Keys at the Tower of London when Robert was commanding the Guard. Nick and Melanie came too and we all went to the officer's flat for a drink beforehand. Julia, for all she was an Air Marshal's daughter, had no great sense of propriety and promptly tried on Robert's bearskin. I was appalled, but Robert thought it great fun.

When the time came, we stood huddled in the dark among the Japanese tourists in front of Traitor's Gate watching the warder with his lamp, keys and escort marching up from the Gatehouse. From over our shoulders out of the dark came the challenge, screamed in thick Glaswegian.

'Halt, hoo gaes there?'

The Japanese jumped in unison and one of the doll-like women giggled. Before the warder's answer came, Nick in best educated Edinburgh accent said, 'I think he must be a Scots Guardsman!' After the ceremony we went back for another drink and watched the television news. By this time Argentina had invaded the Falkland Islands, and the Task Force of Marines and Paras had already set sail for the South Atlantic, but the news was mainly United Nations and diplomatic moves and talk. Robert was restless as usual.

'I should be down there in the Falklands, not guarding these bloody jewels,' he said. We smiled and listened, trying hard not to be condescending. I honestly thought it would all be over by the time the Task Force got there and I said so. Robert was not so sure and was not really amused, but there was nevertheless a twinkle in his eye as he said to his mother, 'I'm a trained killer, you know, every bit as good as these Marines and Paras. I'm sick to death of hearing about Marines and bloody Paras!'

Three days later he was on preparatory training in the Brecon Beacons.

A *BOY'S OWN*
EXISTENCE

Robert Lawrence

I hated the Army at school. I joined the Naval Cadet
Force at Fettes only because it seemed the biggest skive
of the three. After doing that for the absolute minimum
period, I joined the Royal Electrical and Mechanical Engi-
neers because they had a go-kart and a couple of cars.
Eventually, after doing a handbrake corner in a Mor-
ris 1000 on the school drive, spraying a master with
gravel, I got kicked out of the Corps. The head of
the Corps told me I should never go near any of the
armed forces, because I was totally incapable of being
disciplined.

I then went in for the Duke of Edinburgh's Award
Scheme — bronze, then straight on to gold. You had to
do something at school on Wednesday afternoons. There
was a lot of hill-walking in the freezing cold, but I actually
enjoyed it. I think I passed because I had the audacity to
stick with it. There were lots of guys who were fitter and
stronger than I was, who would tear along up front and
then suddenly collapse, whereas I would go along moaning
and moaning — but never stop. And it was the same story
throughout my Army career.

At sixteen I decided to join the Scots Guards, like Chris
my eldest brother before me. He was a very good soldier,
and his reputation hung over my shoulder throughout my
time in the Army. Once, in the early days on Brigade
Squad, when I was crying my eyes out as I dug some
ghastly trench, a Scots Guards sergeant came along and
said, 'If your fucking brother could see you now, sir...'
And it went on from there.

I saw my time in the Army as an opportunity to have a bit of a *Boy's Own* existence. The big thing that also appealed to me about it was that everything I did in the Army *mattered*. Every decision I made as a young man mattered. There are eighteen-year-olds running around in Northern Ireland, for instance, and if they make the wrong decision over something, someone else could get blown up tomorrow in Belfast or London. In a way, I think I also saw the Army as a transition period from school to the real world; I certainly wasn't ready for an office job.

In July 1977, I turned up at the Army's Central London Recruiting Depot for the first time, and was turned away for being too young — under seventeen and a half. Seven months later, I was back again to receive the Queen's shilling which, owing to inflation, was then more like £3.60. Coming out of the dressing room after my medical, wearing just a towelling dressing-gown and socks, I met this strange character called Mark Mathewson. A tall, slim young guy with glasses, about a year older than me and an Old Etonian, he said he was also joining the Scots Guards. We went off to have a drink together with our Queen's shillings, not realizing how our paths would cross again and again, up to the Falklands War and beyond.

Two months later, we went on to Brigade Squad at Pirbright, bundled off the train and on to the Guards Depot in the back of a four-tonner by two lance sergeants. Basically, what they do in Brigade Squad, over eight weeks, is push you to your absolute limit to see what you're made of. My eldest brother Chris avoided it by being recruited via a new Army scheme which took him on straight after university. He went into the Scots Guards after taking a law degree at Cambridge.

During Brigade Squad, we had one weekend off in the middle. The rest of the time they had the right to bug us around twenty-four hours a day. It was classic Army stuff, weapons training, kit-cleaning, learning to march and drill. They could keep us up until 3 a.m. in the morning and then suddenly say, 'Right. Bed. Thirty seconds!' And in thirty seconds we had to be in bed. Then at 5.30 a.m. or 6 a.m. the lance sergeants would come in, smashing the bed with sticks and screaming that we had to be straight up and out again.

We had to learn regimental history — how many VCs were won in the First World War, when Lord Lisle won his VC, and so on. They'd drill it into us every evening for about two hours. They were beating the daylights out of us to see when we'd break. Twenty-six of us started and only about eight of us finally passed. Some guys cracked. I remember once, when we were running up a sand hill on a disused range, with packs on our backs, this chap suddenly collapsed; he lay there, saying, 'I want to die. Someone kill me. I can't bear this any more,' and I couldn't blame him at all. I remember all but cracking up myself once, and a trained soldier came up to me and said, 'You know, if I had my way, I wouldn't give you this hard a time.' But I knew very well he would. We were in fear of everything while we were there. We had to understand that we could never stop and think to ourselves, 'Don't be silly, this guy isn't going to do me physical harm,' because chances were he would.

From what I've heard, Brigade Squad has now been somewhat modified, owing to pressure from parents and so on. But it was a way of sorting out the good from the bad. It was a stubborn streak in me, I think, that kept me going; that, and being so young. I was capable of taking the knocks and the bashes and the ordering around. Being the youngest in my family also meant I was used to being bossed around. If I had been twenty-three, say, as one guy at Brigade Squad was, then I know now that I couldn't have done it.

There were some good moments, though, during the eight weeks. Mark Mathewson, who had the bed next to mine, became a good friend. And I remember a time when Lance Sergeant McGowan, who had known Chris well, suddenly came into our room one day, physically dragged us out of bed by our throats, took us into the lavatories and threw us both into a cubicle. We thought he was going to beat the shit out of us. But instead he put his hand inside his combat jacket, pulled out a can of McEwan's lager, said, 'Don't tell anyone I've given you this,' and shut the door behind us. The Army way.

When I finally finished Brigade Squad, I felt totally and utterly invincible. You come out of that place feeling fifteen foot tall. Soon after that I went on to do the Regular Commissions Board at Westbury — three days of written, oral and command tests: 'Here's a twelve-foot gap and you've got a ten-foot plank, two bits of string and a toothbrush and you've got to get a barrel and your eight men across it' — that sort of thing. If you're Mark Mathewson, you start working out Einstein's theory of relativity and how to string up a suspension bridge; if you're me, you just jump.

At the beginning of January 1979, I went to Sandhurst. After Brigade Squad, it was an absolute doddle as far as I was concerned. I never became a cadet corporal, cadet sergeant or whatever, I just had a good time. I once got dragged in by my company commander and reprimanded for going out too much; barring the nights we were on exercise, he reckoned I'd spent only two nights at Sandhurst during the whole of the second term. In fact I had been found out only because I had always signed the book, as regulations — quite reasonably in my view — required. But in the end I did perfectly well, passed out and went to join the battalion at Chelsea Barracks.

Here, there were all sorts of what I saw as petty initiations, such as the one whereby no senior officer would talk to a new officer for the first few months. However, there was a lot of fun to be had in performing public duties. The first time I ever mounted guard at Buckingham Palace, someone wired a little electric alarm clock into the top of my bearskin which went off at exactly the time I was due to march through the forecourt — *bleep, bleep, bleep!* It was all quite a gas. And then of course there was the social life in London, the invitations to debs' balls and so on.

The Army is very competitive, and I liked competing within it, but what I was not prepared to take part in was the sort of social competition that went on among young men outside it. Look at my car. How much is your private income? Look at this. Look at that. It just never stopped, at the parties and the balls. And I was thoroughly bored by it. I hated that part of a Guards officer's life, that stratum of society whose members have to show off the cars and flats that Daddy has produced for them. Of course, I enjoyed a lot of the glamour of London society, and do now, but I still preferred the excitement of soldiering.

That was to come in April 1980, with a six-and-a-half-month emergency tour of Belfast. Prior to that, we were trained for Northern Ireland in mock villages which the Army build for the purpose. Gurkhas would pretend to be rioters, but were pretty serious about it. One hit me across the side of the head with a baseball bat and burst one of my eardrums, despite the fact that I had a steel helmet on. In the main we were taught that we could never win. For example, the old puddle principle. On patrol, we were told always to go against human nature and walk through a puddle, because if the enemy wants to get someone, he puts an anti-personnel mine on either side of it, where people would normally tread. Knowing that the British Army teaches such principles, the enemy starts mining the centre of puddles — a no-win situation. It was extremely good training, though, and obviously a lot more sophisticated than this might suggest.

Northern Ireland was a very, very, unpleasant place; a lot of unpleasant things happened there. We lived in camps, which we could never leave on our own, and in six and a half months we got only four days off. Every other day we were doing twenty-four-hour duty stints. Day and night we couldn't get undressed, and we patrolled the streets for hours on end. There were riots, house searches for terrorists, constant danger and hostility. Even the dogs there were trained to attack us.

There is no sense of reality about serving in Northern Ireland. On the other hand, it was one hell of an experience for a guy of nineteen, as I was then. I felt that what I did was very important.

On my four days' leave from Belfast, I remember being very jumpy. I went shopping for food in the King's Road on one of those days, when a car suddenly backfired. The minute it did, I dropped those carrier bags and flung myself to the ground in a shop doorway. Of course, everyone looked at me as though I were crazy, rolling around the shop. But I reckoned I'd rather be seen as a bit stupid than be hit by a bullet.

After Belfast came a marvellous spell in Brunei on a Jungle Warfare Instructors' Course, which I really loved. When I came back, I wanted to work in undercover intelligence in Northern Ireland. It was the kind of work that appealed to me. But I had to set it aside when something more immediate suddenly cropped up.

In the spring of 1982, the Commanding Officer announced one day that he was going to speak to us all in the gymnasium. We were bracing ourselves for something to do with the Major General's inspection — a ghastly regular occurrence. But instead he said we were going to the Falklands; there was time only for a quick visit to my parents, plus a crash refresher course in Wales, and then I was gone.

THE VOYAGE SOUTH

Robert Lawrence

The *QE2* was heavily overcrowded with the whole of 5 Brigade, Scots and Welsh Guards, Gurkhas and a lot of support units, when we left for the Falklands from Southampton on 12 May. There were four to a cabin and every inch of space was used. Mark Mathewson and I slept on the floor of the two-person cabin occupied by Simon Price, the company commander, and Ian Bryden, the company second-in-command.

Every single landing on each stairway was used for training. Soldiers running round the outside deck to keep fit hammered the top deck of the *QE2* down by a foot. In the middle of a lecture some little Gurkha would suddenly appear round the corner, wearing his life jacket and a blindfold and feeling his way round the walls, doing lifeboat training. The ladies' toilet was put to use as an intelligence briefing room.

It was surreal, and there were all sorts of interesting little rumours flying around, including one that we had a submarine literally shadowing the *QE2* underneath us, because it was a good way to smuggle it in without its being spotted. We heard at one stage that the Argentinian parliament had been debating whether or not to send out a flight of their best fighter aircraft, Super Etendards, to find the defenceless *QE2* and destroy it, even though the pilots would have had to ditch because they would not have had enough fuel to return to base. In the event, the Argentinians decided that this mission would not be worth the cost. Thank God for that. Imagine how many thousands could have been killed.

Overall, our feelings on the journey down to the Falklands were mixed. We swung, at times, from being desperately scared of the realities of going to war to being just as desperately worried that we'd get down there merely to be told we were just garrisoning the islands — and that the Marines had more or less done all the work. At other times, we thought that the UN might call it all off, and that we'd have to go back home.

I remember writing my last letter home to my parents. It was a bit like one of those 1940s Richard Todd movies, a young man writing his last letter home before he went to war.

And this is a very interesting aspect of war, I think, since the advent of television. Something that people in Vietnam perhaps also experienced; the idea of this big circle, where people going to war find themselves acting as they have seen people act in films about people going to war. Living how you expect you should be living. Writing in your letters what you have seen people in films writing in their last letters home.

I knew my parents were worried, naturally, and I remember saying something vaguely along the lines that they should bear in mind, in the future, when normal everyday frustrations infuriated them and got them worked up, what it was like now, when there was a real problem, when the reality of the situation was that I was going to war, and might never come back alive. In comparison to that, things like the car not starting sort of pale into insignificance. Only, of course, none of us was to realize the poignancy of words like these until much later.

* * *

The QE2 finished its journey, about three weeks later, at South Georgia, a long distance from the Falklands, but safe territory, as the SAS had already cleared the island of Argentinians, though all credit for it seemed to go to the Marines. Cunard were desperately anxious that their flagship be spared the threat of Argentinian attack, and so at South Georgia we were transferred on to the *Canberra* which took us to San Carlos Water, otherwise known as 'bomb alley'.

I had the front top berth on the *Canberra*, which is about the worst place to be. Every time the ship lurched with the waves, a cupboard door with a broken latch swung open and the automatic light inside the cupboard came on. Then, as the ship wallowed again, the cupboard door swung shut. This went on all through the night. It was like sleeping in some wretched Third World mobile discothèque.

Outside, meanwhile, the weather was getting progressively colder. There were enormous blue and turquoise icebergs floating around, and flotillas of penguins in the middle of nowhere. It was like something out of a Jules Verne movie — spectacular, but also dream-like.

When we arrived at the Falkland Islands some days later, the temperature was freezing, aggravated by a severe wind chill factor. I remember that one of the first sights that impressed me most was a Harrier jump-jet landing on an aircraft-carrier. One minute this extremely fast, streamlined machine was hurtling along, and the next it suddenly slowed down in mid-air and floated down to the ship's deck. There was something strangely beautiful about it.

Landing craft took us ashore from San Carlos Water, and we then trudged up the hillside quite a long way until we were assigned individual areas and dug ourselves into a defensive position. We had been supplied with quite a bit of information by then, including the fact that our British Forces Post Office number for the Falklands was 666. A lot of people got quite panicked about that —— 666 being the mark of the devil.

I recall that we were also issued with the common passwords for recognition purposes: 'Jimmy' for the Scots Guards and 'Johnny' for the Gurkhas. The reason for this was that the Argentinians couldn't pronounce the J, and would come up with 'himmy' or 'hohnny'. It struck us as rather amusing.

During one orders group, I remember being told to tune in to a certain frequency on our radios to pick up the BBC World Service. This, we were informed, would tell us exactly what was happening on the islands, and where we were to be fighting. So much for war in the 1980s, the age of sophisticated modern communications!

Living in a hole on the San Carlos beachhead, meanwhile, was not particularly pleasant. The minute we dug a hole, it filled up with freezing water, which we then had to sleep in. Not nice, but then that's what soldiers are meant to do. At the end of two days, we were asked to make our three-day ration packs last six days. By then, however, it was a bit late, as we'd already eaten two-thirds of them. It was something that caused, I recall, a touch of disillusionment and upset.

Early in June, we were taken to Fitzroy in landing craft, and then had a long march to Bluff Cove. The weather was horrific, and what with people stripped down for a march constantly having to stop and start again in the cold, hypothermia and other problems began to set in.

Sutherland, one of my Guardsmen, was suffering badly at the time. I ordered him to come and share a trench with me, so that I could keep an eye on him, but was then called to an orders group down at some sheep huts. By the time I got back, Sutherland was lying in the dark in this hole full of water, and had stopped breathing. His heart had also stopped. I gave him artificial respiration and a cardiac massage to get him going again and started screaming for help to try to get him out.

His heart kept stopping as we carried him out and I continued giving him artificial respiration; then he threw up in my mouth. At one point I picked him up by his hair and kicked him in the back as hard as I possibly could to get him going again. Eventually they took him to the hospital at Fitzroy. But no sooner was he bedded down than the *Sir Galahad* was hit and he had to be out of bed again and helping. In the Army, you're only ever as ill as the situation allows you to be.

We saw the *Galahad* hit from the hill we were standing on. The Argentinian planes that had hit her came screaming over our heads fast and low — faster than the speed of sound, so you didn't hear them until they were right upon you. The whole battalion, about six hundred people, began firing at them, putting up a solid wall of lead. It was like being at the fairground.

In the end, we brought down three of them, and then we ran to the top of the hill to see what was happening below. The *Galahad* was a horrific sight. Only later were we to realize the scandal that lay behind her getting hit and how a ship full of troops should never have been left unprotected like that, vulnerable to air attack. For the time being, though, the event merely reinforced the thought in our heads that here we were, actually at war, and things were going to keep happening. It made us strive to keep on going.

Soon after the *Galahad* incident, we started getting information about the possibility of an attack on Tumbledown, and began to prepare for the battle that was to tip the balance in the Falklands War.

FOREBODING

John Lawrence

The days that followed Robert's departure were tense to
say the least. We dared not miss a news bulletin and as the
fighting at sea began, we were more and more on edge.
The Marines and Paras landed at San Carlos Bay and we
got a letter from Robert via Ascension Island. It mentioned
the possibility of a submarine attack and Jean bit her lip as
she read it, but said nothing. 'Oh please God let it finish
before he gets there. Really? Do I mean that? He will be
impossible if the Marines and Paras finish it before he
can have a go. God, give him strength, and courage and
cheerfulness.'

Despite the war, I still had my job to do as Assistant
Secretary of the MCC, and June was a busy month. The
day the Lord's Test Match began, I left home as usual
at seven, before the papers arrived. The MCC members'
queue was already past the Tavern as I drove in through
the Grace Gates. Among the newspaper placards advertis-
ing the various cricket writers and their columns I caught
a glimpse of 'Guards in Hell'. I parked quickly and rushed
into the committee room. The reports of the attack on the
Sir Galahad were brief in the extreme and although they
talked about Guards, none said whether they were Scots
or Welsh. The next day we still did not know.

Her Majesty the Queen comes on the Friday of the
Test Match if she is able to come at all, and in 1982
we were delighted when we learned that she would be
coming that year. We always line up to be presented —
the Trustees, the Officers, the Committee and at the end
the Secretariat. When Billy Griffith had been President he

had caused some amusement in the introductions. He was very nervous and when he got to the Secretariat he said, 'Ma'am, this is Lieutenant-Colonel Stephenson, he is an Assistant Secretary. And this is Lieutenant-Colonel James, he is an Assistant Secretary. And this is Wing Commander, er, and he's another one!' There had always been a healthy rivalry between the Army and the RAF. Occasionally it went too far. In the face of this, during the Second World War, the Air Ministry decreed that Army officers were not to be referred to as 'pongos'. The Admiralty, on the other hand, considering themselves to be above this, issued an order that pongos were to be referred to as Army officers. That put the Army in their place, I chuckled to myself as I recalled hearing that story — and then I remembered I had two sons in the Scots Guards.

This year, for the first time that I can remember, a member of the Secretariat was allowed to spend a few minutes sitting with the Queen in the window. It is a ritual normally orchestrated by the President and the Secretary, who select members of the Committee and, if available, players from the touring side to rotate through the chairs on either side of Her Majesty. To my astonishment, on that day Hubert Doggart, the President, ushered me in to sit on her left while Jim Swanton was eased in on her right.

I had met the Queen before, when the All Blacks rugby team had gone to Buckingham Palace, and of course I had been presented in the committee room line-up several times before, but this was very different. I realized that the chances of getting a word in with Jim in the other chair were very slim, but suddenly the Falklands came up. 'Oh, I have a son in the Falklands, Ma'am,' I blurted out. The Queen immediately seemed interested only in what I had to say. She is marvellous, I think, in the way she is able to show interest in everything and everyone, but I felt this was a different interest. She mentioned Prince Andrew and I suddenly realized that, although she was the Queen and I her servant, in that moment we were almost on a par, parents concerned for the welfare of our children.

The Queen talked to me for some time and told me
it had been Welsh Guards not Scots Guards on the *Sir
Galahad*. I explained how badly I felt to experience such
relief at the expense of someone else and I thought briefly
of Welsh mothers and fathers who would be getting bad
news soon. The Queen understood completely; after all,
more than one Sea King helicopter had been lost.

We had family friends, the Harveys, staying with us
for the Test Match and on Saturday night Duncan and I
had our usual session after dinner on the malt whisky and
Corries records, but Jean and Ann would not leave us as
they usually did, insisting on staying up with us and talking
over the music. One song in particular, however, which
we knew to be Robert's platoon song, had us all listening
together:

I will go, I will go
When the fighting is over
To the land of Macleod
That I left to be a soldier
I will go, I will go.

When we landed on the shore
And saw the foreign heather
We knew that some would fall
And would stay there for ever.

When we came back to the glen
Winter was turning
Our goods lay in the snow
And our houses were burning
I will go, I will go.

The next morning in church, Jean had to leave in the
middle of the first hymn. She had no idea why she was
crying other than a general worry about Robert. I offered
to go with her but she insisted on going alone. She was
better at lunch time, but I knew it was only a brave face.
The Harveys left in mid-afternoon, and after the early

evening news and a light supper we went to bed. Tommy, the dachshund, was not amused at being made to have an early night. At about eleven o'clock I went down to him and found him out of his bed, wandering about the kitchen. I let him out, but he was not really interested. After a good sniff round he came back in whimpering. I put him in his bed and tried to settle him down, stroking him and talking to him. I could not understand what might be wrong.

Four times in the night I woke to hear Tommy crying softly, but when I went down to him, only once was he walking around. The other times he appeared to be dreaming. In the morning I took him in the car to work as usual and thought nothing more of it. Only later did I learn it was the night of the battle for Tumbledown.

TUMBLEDOWN
MOUNTAIN

Robert Lawrence

The battle for Tumbledown Mountain was set for the night of 13 / 14 June. I heard later that the original brigade plan had been to attack by day. Had we done that, there is no doubt in my mind that the Argentinians would have killed us all on the approach; their positions on the other side — the Stanley side — of Mount Tumbledown were very strong. Following their defeat by the Paras at Darwin and Goose Green about a fortnight earlier, these positions were the Argentinians' last ring of close defence, and were on very high ground outside Port Stanley. To finish the job in the Falklands, it was obviously vital for us to attack these final positions and take them.

Helicopters took us initially up to Goat Ridge, and from here a valley separated us from Tumbledown. Almost as soon as we had begun to dig in, we came under Argentinian artillery bombardment, which was quite something. The Argentinians had no observation posts to see precisely where their shells were landing; they were just hoping to hit British troops at some point. Listening to our casualty reports over their radios would tell them when they'd hit someone, and indicate where they should concentrate their fire.

A shell landed by the trench occupied by Sergeant McGeorge and Corporal Campbell, who were in my company. Corporal Campbell had taken his webbing off to dig, and it caught fire, sending white phosphorous grenades everywhere, which everyone thought was rather funny at the time. And then Sergeant McGeorge got a piece of shrapnel up his arse, which everyone thought was even funnier; Sergeant McGeorge, such a warrior-like guy, having to be pulled out of battle because of a piece of shrapnel up his bum.

During that day, we continued to come under quite heavy shelling, but we also got the chance to crawl up the hill above us, in separate groups, and saw Tumbledown just vaguely in the distance. And through our binoculars we could see the Argentinian position that we were going to attack.

Despite slight nerves at this point, morale was fairly high. We had a sense that we were actually about to go and do a real job. Up until then, our biggest fear had been that we were going to have to spend more weeks sitting around in trenches, becoming progressively colder and more miserable.

We came across some Paras who had been at Goose Green and Darwin earlier. I grabbed one and couldn't resist asking, 'What's it like?'

'Um,' he said, 'it's pretty nasty, but get within two hundred metres of them and they'll run away. And if you hit a machine-gun sangar with an anti-tank weapon, it will stop.'

I believed all that, right until we actually got up on to Tumbledown. It was only then that we discovered that the troops the Paras had fought and captured at Goose Green, in the Argentinians' outer ring of defence, were mostly teenage conscripts. The troops we were to face at Tumbledown, however, were extremely well-trained and well-equipped marines in their mid-twenties, who had had recent fighting experience in the Argentinian civil war. They had had years of aggression. They were well used to it. People like me, on the other hand, only weeks previously had been doing the Changing of the Guard at Buckingham Palace — not exactly the greatest experience for fighting a war in some godforsaken little island in the middle of nowhere.

The battalion battle plan was basically that Tumbledown would be divided into thirds. G Company, one of the rifle companies in the Scots Guards, would take on the first third. Left Flank, another rifle company, would then take the middle third, and Right Flank, which was my company, would take the last third, the end part.

Once again, we were faced with a familiar worry, that G Company and Left Flank would overrun the entire position and leave us with nothing to do. We had been told that there was a machine-gun post at the foot of Tumbledown, plus about a battalion of Argentinians, and that they were very, very good.

At night, we crossed the start line on Goat Ridge, and I met up with the Adjutant, Mark Bullough. He had a walking-stick with him. Again, I thought, it was the classic sort of eccentricity you expect to see in war films.

'Hello, Robert,' he said, poking me in the chest. 'You do well, but keep your head down.'

We shook out into our positions and came under artillery and mortar fire. Shells whistled over our heads and, because it was night, we could see the flash of their explosion before we heard the bang, which meant that everyone ended up ducking at totally the wrong time. By the time we were ducking for the bang, the shell had already gone off.

The Scots Guards first mounted a diversionary attack towards Mount William, to make the Argentinians think that this would be the direction we would be coming from. Major Richard Bethel went off on this with various odds and sods he'd managed to get together, people from battalion headquarters, and one of my Guardsmen who had trench foot. Having earlier been told he couldn't take part in the battle because of the handicap, he was suddenly grabbed back again for this exercise, trench foot or not.

Richard planned to get his men to a position about two or three hundred yards away from the Argentinians, and then to open fire on them like hell, whether he was killing them or not, to cause the diversion. But when he reached his chosen spot and looked through his individual weapon sight (IWS) which enabled him to see at night, he couldn't see any Argentinians.

He and his men carried on a bit further, but still couldn't see where the Argentinians were. A bit further on, however, he suddenly heard snoring and, looking down, saw that there were three Argentinian trenches right in front of him. They had walked right up to them.

Unfortunately, at that moment a loud radio signal blasted out over Richard's headset. The first Argentinian to wake up opened fire with his FN rifle on automatic and killed Drill Sergeant Danny Wight with a bullet through the forehead, Danny who only weeks earlier had been on the Ceremony of the Keys with me. The Argentinian also put two bullets through Richard's hood and killed the Royal Engineer sergeant who had been on Richard's left. Richard opened up with a bren gun, but one Argentinian, even while being riddled with bullets, managed to get a grenade out, which put shrapnel up Richard's leg and cut his jacket clean in half, like a knife.

Richard turned to pick up Danny, who was about six foot eight, and started running out with his other men as more Argentinians woke up and began firing at them. They ran into a minefield, where Danny had to be left. And my Guardsman with trench foot got rid of his trench foot as quickly as you can imagine by standing on a mine and having his leg blown off.

That was the diversionary attack. It was in fact very successful.

The first third of Tumbledown — G Company's — seemed to have no Argentinians on it at all. For ages no fighting started in front of us and we thought, oh no, here we go again. We're going to get on to Tumbledown and there aren't going to be any Argentinians there.

Then Left Flank started doing their central third and were faced with extreme fighting, the worst sort of resistance you can imagine — hand-to-hand fighting, bayonets, the works — and seven of their men were killed. Eventually, they fought their way through their third, commanded by Major John Kiszely, who did an incredible job in those horrific circumstances and subsequently won a Military Cross. This had been out-and-out battle, the fullest possible fighting, and constituted the main part of the battle for Tumbledown.

I was somewhere at the back of all this, wondering what the hell was going on. It was bloody cold. Really, really cold, so cold that I thought I was going to die. I remember at one stage not being able to move because of it, not being able to motivate myself to keep moving, and I just sat behind a rock getting colder and colder.

Then my platoon sergeant came along and started kicking the boys and kicking me to get us going again. I honestly think I would have died if it hadn't been for him.

Left Flank were eventually stopped by a well-placed multiple machine-gun post that was in Right Flank's third of the mountain. A friend of mine, Lieutenant Alastair Mitchell, was machine-gunned through the legs. Now, having done an incredible job, and with so many men injured and a number killed, Left Flank had to stop.

Right Flank were called up to join them. As we were making our way along, we found a dead Scots Guardsman. His body had been marked by a rifle stuck in the ground with a beret placed on top of it. It was harrowing. But it also made us angry, and inspired us to push on all the harder.

Stumbling over the scree, I suddenly came across some Argentinian tents which didn't seem to have been cleared by Left Flank — at least, there weren't any holes in them. I decided to check them over myself and I cut open the sides with my bayonet. Inside they stank to high heaven, as if humans had been living in them for months. BO and socks and worse.

We discovered boxes of highly sophisticated night sights in the tents, which we hadn't believed the Argentinians had. Time and again we'd been told how poorly equipped they were supposed to be, yet here were third-generation

IWSs, the absolute top grade, more advanced than the ones we had ourselves. It made us wonder again what lay ahead.

At long last we were moving into battle and were going to have an opportunity to put our training into practice. By this time, any anxiety we had felt earlier that the Argentinians might not be there — or, at least, that we would not have a chance to meet them in combat — had not only vanished, but seemed utterly ridiculous. On the contrary, in fact, our fear now was that there were Argentinian snipers concealed in the crags up to our left — possibly equipped with night sights from the very boxes we had just discovered in their tents.

It was all very disorientating. One minute we'd be scrambling along, not knowing when or where we'd find the guys from Left Flank we were supposed to be joining, and the next minute they'd just appear out of nowhere.

After a while we met a number of men from Left Flank, among them the brilliant Major John Kiszely. There he stood with his silver-white hair all lit up by the dazzling starlight shells. These special illuminating devices were fired up by the Navy, to descend very slowly on parachutes. They gave off an incredible light and, as they fell lower in the sky, produced longer and increasingly bizarre shadows.

In addition to all this, there was a fierce snow blizzard blowing. And John Kiszely, who had done quite a lot of hand-to-hand fighting by then and had also been shot at, only to have the bullet lodge itself in his compass, just stood there, I remember, all enthusiastic and looking like the Monarch of the Glen.

At that moment I forgot the cold. I was extremely excited. And I made up my mind then that I would never, later, be saying to myself, 'If only I'd done this or that at the time'. I was really going to go for it. Yes, I told myself, what the fuck, I am really going to go for it now.

* * *

I myself, my company commander Simon Price, plus the two other platoon commanders, Mark Mathewson and

James Dalrymple, were all briefed by Major Kiszely on the Argentinian machine-gun post which lay ahead. And we decided on a right-flanking attack.

I led off to a gully to the right with my platoon in front, and Mark's followed behind. One of the big problems, of course, in doing a right-hand attack was that, not knowing where the enemy were, we could end up, when we finally turned in left, either too far in front of them or too far behind. It was essential to turn precisely where they were, and hit them from the side.

Not far down the gully, I collected a rifle with an IWS on it, saw some Argentinians moving position across the back of Tumbledown, and picked off about four of them. I then radioed to James Dalrymple's platoon, who were joining Left Flank to add fire protection, and asked them to put some fire down on the Argentinian machine-gun post, so that we could see where it was. I also hoped their fire would keep the Argentinians' heads down while we came in on the attack.

The minute we started leading our assault in, however, the machine-gun post saw us coming, and switched its fire on to us. We hit the ground at about the time Mark's platoon was coming up level with us, and then tried to return fire. I began crawling forward on my own for about forty or fifty feet, and remember feeling desperately scared. There were bullets flying everywhere — from James's platoon on my left, from the Argentinians ahead, and from my own guys behind, and the bullets were all ricocheting off the rocks. This is it, I thought. This is the end. And, as I continued to crawl along, I tried to make myself disappear into the ground, face right down in the dirt.

Eventually I got behind a rock and attempted to pull the pin out of a white phosphorous grenade. I had never used such a grenade before, and discovered that they have very heavy-duty pins. I should have ensured that they had been pre-prepared with a pair of pliers so I could get the bloody things out. Instead I had to crawl back again, under all this fire, to Corporal Simpson. He held the pin, I held the grenade, and together we got the thing out. Holding the safety lever of the grenade down, I then had to crawl all the way back to my original position, and screamed at my men to reduce their fire. Then I hurled the thing into the air, and the grenade went straight into the machine-gun post and blew up.

I took off, and screamed at my men to follow me. In that instant, my one sudden thought was, are they going to follow me, or will I be left to run off on my own? But when I glanced round, there was this unbelievably fantastic sight of every man getting up and running in. I remember thinking at that moment that this was life on a knife edge. Amazing. Fantastic. Nothing would ever bother me again from then on. If I got back to London and found that my flat had burned down, it would be a totally insignificant event in comparison to this experience.

The other thing that occurred to me was that people just don't die in real life the way they do on television. If a man is shot, a bit of him might come off, but he doesn't drop immediately. He just carries on coming. It takes an enormous amount to kill a man. Usually he has to be shot three or four times before he dies.

As well as being told that the Argentinians were ill-equipped, we had also been led to believe that they were starving. This was another myth. In the first Argentinian trench I came across, cans and cans of food had been poured into the bottom, just to keep the occupiers' feet out of the water. And the other thing these Argentinians didn't do, as we'd been informed they did, was run away.

There were numerous Argentinians in the machine-gun post. They were wearing American-style uniform: big green parkas with webbing over the top. I remember searching my first prisoner frantically for a Colt 45 pistol, because I desperately wanted one as a souvenir to take back to England.

The horrible thing about having your first prisoner is that it's rather like being a man with a snake. Snakes are quite probably more terrified of humans than humans can ever believe they are. The same applies to prisoners. I was terrified that the prisoner might suddenly do something fast and clever and kill me, or that he would do something that meant I would have to kill him. There's an appalling tension, a feeling that at any minute the horror could all suddenly erupt again.

There were panics when we asked Argentinians to put their hands up and they went on clutching their rifles in the pandemonium. We'd scream, 'Drop your fucking rifle!' But they didn't understand us.

Just as the assault appeared to have come to a grinding halt, and we were dealing with the wounded and the prisoners, we suddenly came under sniper fire from the crags above us. There was a danger we'd all get picked off there and then, so we moved away. I grabbed two of my Guardsmen, and we set off to go round the Stanley end of Tumbledown. We stepped round a craggy rock — and then the whole bloody world seemed to explode.

Gunfire, grenades, explosions, booby traps maybe, everything erupted on the other side of this rock, so we quickly jumped back again. Guardsman Pengelly, who was with me, started climbing up the rocks to try to reach the top and get at one of the sniper positions. As he was climbing, he was hit and fell back down again, wounded but not killed. I felt I had to keep the momentum going. I grabbed two or three people, including Corporal Rennie and Sergeant McDermot, and went round the other end of the rock, and we started skirmishing down — one guy moving on while the other covered him. Again, I remember thinking that this was just like the movies.

By now it was just becoming daylight and, among the grass and rocks, I saw an Argentinian lying face down, with his arms back. I thought to myself, is he dead or alive? But instead of just kicking or prodding him, I stuck my bayonet into the back of his arm, dug it right in because I had run out of ammunition. He spun wildly on the ground, and my bayonet snapped. And as he spun, he was trying to get a Colt 45 out of an army holster on his waist. So I had to stab him to death. I stabbed him and I stabbed him, again and again, in the mouth, in the face, in the guts, with a snapped bayonet.

It was absolutely horrific. Stabbing a man to death is not a clean way to kill somebody, and what made it doubly horrific was that at one point he started screaming '*Please. . .*' in English to me. But had I left him he could have ended up shooting me in the back.

When I did finally leave him, I took his FN rifle, moved on, shot a sniper, picked up his FN and moved on again. I was moving on with other men when suddenly Guardsman McEntaggart turned to me and said, 'Excuse me, sir, I think I've been shot.'

I thought, don't be stupid, if you've been shot you'd know all about it. He had in fact been grazed by a bullet in the upper arm.

I still desperately wanted to push on at this stage and get to an Argentinian administration and supply area, at the very end of Tumbledown. Once we had taken that, we would have taken the whole mountain. It was also in the direction of Stanley — the goal we were all heading for.

Men from the different platoons behind me were dealing with the wounded and prisoners, but I was aware, as I moved along, of other people coming up behind me, taking various routes. Ian Bryden, our company second-in-command, was dashing along the top of the mountain doing all sorts of heroics. Sergeant Jackson handed his rifle and webbing to a Guardsman and went off on his own, with two grenades, to take some Argentinians out. It was all incredible stuff.

I remember seeing the lights of Stanley below us and thinking how strange that it hadn't been blacked out. This was supposed to be a war. I turned to Guardsman McEntaggart as we went along and, for some inexplicable reason, suddenly cried out, 'Isn't this fun?'

Seconds later, it happened. I felt a blast in the back of my head that felt more as if I'd been hit by a train than by a bullet. It was a high-velocity bullet, in fact, travelling at a speed of around 3800 feet per second, and the air turbulence and shock wave travelling with it was what caused so much damage. I found this out later. At the time, all I knew was that my knees had gone and I collapsed, totally paralysed, on to the ground.

FIRST NEWS

John Lawrence

The six o'clock news on Monday, 14 June, showed a British major in the Gurkhas announcing over his radio that white flags were flying over Port Stanley. 'Bloody marvellous,' he said and we were ecstatic, but almost without thinking I said to Jean that there would be a lot of people who were yet to receive bad news as a result of the weekend battles. As usual the Scots Guards were barely mentioned, just Marines and bloody Paras.

The Tuesday morning papers announced the surrender and quietly we gave thanks to God; but I repeated my warning that many were yet to get bad news. Christopher rang during the day to say that he had talked with the Scots Guards orderly room and there was no news other than that the battalion had taken Tumbledown Mountain in the final battle and there had been casualties: seven dead and thirty-nine wounded so far. Robert was not among them. I wanted to feel relief, but could not allow myself to do so.

On Wednesday morning my office door burst open and Christopher appeared. 'It's Robert, Daddy,' he said and burst into tears. 'He's been wounded, but they reckon he'll be all right. It's a gunshot wound to the head, but he's not categorized either seriously or very seriously ill so they think it'll just be a nick.'

We embraced and took strength from each other. Chris had borrowed his boss's car and I followed him as we went off to tell Jean at Westminster College, where she is a senior lecturer.

'We'll go via Chelsea Barracks,' said Chris, 'in case there's more news.'

Half-way down Park Lane a taxi cut across Chris and at the next traffic lights we drew up three abreast. I leaned across to talk, but Chris had got out of the car and was haranguing the taxi driver.

'Don't ever do that to me again or you won't live to regret it. My youngest brother's just been shot and wounded in the Falklands.'

The taxi driver turned pale and apologized meekly. 'I'm sorry, mate, I really am.'

Chris talked us through the gates at Chelsea Barracks and we went straight to the orderly room. I knew the colour sergeant there but was not particularly consoled by his statement that he could have won money on Robert getting hurt. 'He was bound to, sir, we all knew that he'd be up there in the front leading his boys. But don't you worry, sir, it'll just be a nick, he's a survivor, that one.'

The Families Officer came into the room and expressed the same opinion. I had met him before as well and knew that he had been hit in the head by shrapnel when the IRA blew up the Irish Guards bus outside the barracks the previous year. His hair had not grown on the scar, but he seemed to have recovered. That was some consolation, but I could not accept that a 'gunshot wound to head' could possibly be anything but very serious.

At Westminster College the West Indian security guard on the desk rang through for Jean. Chris and I stood waiting apprehensively and when she appeared she knew as soon as she saw us. Her face drained white as she rushed towards us saying, 'It's Robert, isn't it?'

I held her tight and said, 'Yes, he's been wounded, but he'll be all right. He's not categorized and that's very important.'

'Why? Where's he been hit?'

I told her it was a gunshot wound to the head. She almost collapsed. Someone appeared and ushered us into the library. Then we went to her head of department's office where he gave us brandy. It was very kind, but the possibility that Robert had really been terribly badly wounded was beginning to dawn on me, and being with Jean as well as Chris seemed to make it worse. Jean was brave as always, but it was as though she was in a daze, totally stunned by the news.

Finding Nick was a bit of a problem, but eventually we tracked him down to a house in Hammersmith. The door was open and the inside appeared to be virtually gutted. Nick was in the back garden and saw us draw up outside. Planks had been laid through the house for wheelbarrows to take soil through to the garden he was building. We met in the doorway, perched precariously on the plank bridge.

Nick showed little emotion, but embraced his mother and consoled her gently as she told him what had happened. He looked over her shoulder and tears were in his eyes. Chris and I each took one of Jean's hands and the three of us looked at each other, but said not a word. Then we went to the cars to go and tell Melanie.

The next day, Thursday, Jean stayed at home, but I went to Lord's as usual. As we went through the post, opening the ticket and membership applications and the queries about the laws of the game, not much was said. The two colonels had enquired how Robert was, but what could I say? All I could do was go through it all again, 'Gunshot wound to head, not categorized, he was bound to be hurt, he would be up the front there leading his men, it will only be a nick.' Jack Bailey, the Secretary of MCC, did not show up at letter-opening, but when I got to my office he looked in to say how sorry he was to hear my awful news and to tell me to take what time off I needed. What else was there to say? I tried to save him further embarrassment by saying I was sure Robert would be all right. Gunshot wound to head. How could he possibly be all right? Oh God, please give him strength and courage and — cheerfulness? No, the most I could ask for was hope.

Half-way through the morning I was walking through the Long Room when a steward told me there was a colonel to see me in my office. It was the Lieutenant Colonel Commanding Scots Guards. We had not met before, though I knew his two predecessors, so we introduced ourselves and shook hands. I got the distinct impression that shaking hands was not really done. He seemed nervous and I invited him to sit down, but before he did he said, 'I'm afraid he's very seriously ill. We have had a signal this morning categorizing him. Unfortunately, I have no more details.'

I knew from my years in the Royal Air Force that 'very seriously ill' meant that Robert was not expected to live. How often in my days at the RAF Record Office had I been duty officer and had to break such news to parents and wives.

We stood embarrassed as I fought to keep back the tears.

'I'll let you know as soon as we have anything more,' said the Colonel.

'I would be very grateful. When I saw the first signal with Christopher in the orderly room at Chelsea yesterday the colour sergeant said that Robert was not categorized so he was sure it would be just a nick. I knew it would be worse than that. I said that if anyone else on the signal had been categorized I would have accepted it, but apart from Drill Sergeant Wight, who was dead, no one was categorized. Pengelly wasn't categorized and he was in Robert's platoon, wasn't he?'

'Er, I am not sure,' said the Colonel, who looked as though he needed a drink.

I thanked him for taking the trouble to come to tell me personally and showed him out of the pavilion to his staff car.

That day a friend of Jean's, Phyllis Tovar, came up from Gloucester to be with her. Phyl had cancelled a holiday on which she was due to go that weekend and I believe it cost her quite a lot of money. It may be a cliché, but at times like these you really do know who your friends are.

On Friday there was still no further news. I had visions of Robert with half a face, with no eye or, worse, totally blind. Would he be a cabbage? Oh God, please let him not be a cabbage. Give him strength and courage and — yes, hope.

In the afternoon I rang the Colonel and insisted that I must know the extent of Robert's injuries. He said he would send a signal to find out. I wondered why I should have had to suggest that he do that.

When I got home, Jean said the GOC had telephoned and she too had complained that we did not know exactly what had happened to Robert and the effect his injury would have on him. I did not explain my understanding of 'very seriously ill'. The next morning the General rang to say the Colonel's signal had crossed with one from the battalion. Robert was suffering from 'left hemiplegia of right penetrating wound'. We told Chris and Nick and deduced that it meant something had gone into the right-hand side of the head, thereby paralysing the left-hand side of the body. Was it a bullet, shrapnel, a bayonet or even a bit of rock? 'Gunshot wound to head,' Chris reminded me.

At about eleven o'clock the father of Melanie's boss rang. We had never met, but he was a neuro-surgeon and was ringing to explain the wording on the signal. It meant what we had thought and he forecast a useless left arm and at best a severe limp, but Robert might never walk again. We thanked the man's disembodied voice down the telephone and sat back, numb, to wait. Cabbage? Oh God, please not that — and please give him courage and strength and hope.

IN TERROR OF DYING

Robert Lawrence

The pain in my head was quite indescribable. The wound was so hot and burning that I wanted to rub it into the mud and snow. But I couldn't move. Only after a little while did any feeling return to my right side. And I remember thinking, oh my God, everybody's going to think I'm dead because I'm not moving, and they're not going to come and help me.

I think Sergeant McDermot was the first to arrive. He took my beret off — headgear the British wore to distinguish them from the Argentinians in their steel helmets — and my head just kept gushing blood. I think Mark Mathewson arrived soon after, and suggested packing snow into the wound, which seemed a pretty good idea. Then I was struck by the awful thought that I had led all my men into a trap, and that most of them would now be dead owing to my stupid foolishness in being too gung-ho.

Then I started worrying about my family back home, and Mitty, my girlfriend at the time. And I started getting very, very panicky about dying. By this stage, I'd lost about five pints of blood, the temperature was sub-zero, the wind chill factor brought it even lower, and there was a fierce blizzard. I was wondering, where are the sleeping bags the platoon were meant to be carrying for casualties, and where the hell was the helicopter that was meant to come and pick me up?

I was getting really irate, and remember looking at Sergeant McDermot and saying, 'Get on your bloody radio and find out where that helicopter is. I'm dying.'

He looked at me, sort of lost, and said, 'My radio isn't working, sir.'

It was all quite ghastly and incredible, but I knew at that point that there was no point in yelling at him. Then, with the fear and frustration, I suddenly began to cry.

Sergeant McDermot came up to me and said, 'Go on, sir, you have a good cry.'

And I thought, you bastard, I'm *not* going to cry. I had been all for crying up to the minute he said that and then I just thought stuff it, I won't.

Soon after that we came under a lot of artillery fire from Stanley, and Mark Mathewson screamed at everyone to get away from me, because we had obviously been spotted. He was absolutely right. There was no point in everyone else dying. Sergeant Oakes, the medical sergeant, stayed with me, though, plus a couple of the others, and they lay on top of me to try and keep me warm.

While they were doing that, as I found out later, an enormous artillery shell landed about six feet away from all of us, sank itself into the soil, but didn't go off. Had it done so, none of us would be here today.

Finally, after over two hours, the helicopter arrived. The air crewman, a guy called Jay, together with Sergeant Oakes, got me over to it and into the back. Again, something I found out later was that the pilot of this Scout helicopter, Captain Sammy Drennan, shouldn't really have been there as he was over the line on his map that he had been told not to cross. Sammy had been a Scots Guards colour sergeant before transferring to the Army Air Corps, and apparently when he heard about the number of casualties his old regiment was suffering, he decided he'd go in and get some out if he could. Had he been shot down in the process — for undoubtedly he was an Argentinian target — he might well have been reprimanded. As it was, he didn't get shot down and he was awarded a Distinguished Flying Cross.

The helicopter was flown in and out of Tumbledown several times very fast, and very, very low. Jay told me that while he and Sammy were doing one particularly horrific flight, attempting to get away without being hit, Sammy suddenly peered down at the sea and said, 'Oh look. A seal.' Jay thought he was mad. Here they were, risking their lives, and Sammy could still worry about seals!

I had lost so much blood during the two and a half hours I'd been waiting on the mountain, it was a wonder I was still alive, and they had no drip on the helicopter. But then again, I was absolutely terrified of dying. I could so easily have gone into shock and died then, full stop. Either that or gone into a coma. But the sheer fear of dying seemed to keep me hanging on.

There wasn't much room in the helicopter, so my head ended up hanging out of the door as we were flying along. Jay tried to hold me up, and he took off his woolly Arctic hat and put it over my head to protect it from the freezing wind. But it immediately blew off again. Sammy was flying at breakneck speed to get us all out.

The pain in my head continued to be agonizing; about forty-five per cent of my brain had been blown away. But I wasn't allowed any morphine or other form of anaesthetic, for fear that it would kill me. I was tempted to give in to the pain, but I was too frightened to.

Years later, when my mother got upset and said things like at least I was still alive, I'd be thinking, what's there to be so grateful for in that? But at the time, in those crucial hours after I was shot, I fought against dying like hell.

* * *

I was flown to the field hospital at Fitzroy, which was a converted refrigeration plant. Casualties were divided into three categories: those they could save if they worked quickly; those they could save but who could afford to wait a bit longer; and those who were probably going to die. Unsurprisingly, perhaps, I was put on a drip and stuck at the back of the queue in the last category.

The system made sense. There was no point spending six and a half hours working on a man who was going to die when, during that time, three might die and four get worse who could have been saved with prompt attention.

I waited four and a half hours there — this on top of the two and a half hours I'd already spent on the mountain — and still wasn't allowed any anaesthetic. The first thing they did, though, was remove my clothes, to check that I didn't have any injuries underneath that were not visible. Something like a piece of shrapnel, for instance, which could be piercing my heart or a lung.

I remember feeling vaguely annoyed about the way they were doing it — cutting straight through the leather of my best Northern Ireland boots with a gigantic pair of scissors, rather than just cutting the laces, and tearing into my best SAS Arctic smock. I'd put on all my best stuff to go into battle; a bit like gearing up to go to a disco on a Friday night. It was very typical of me, because most other people didn't do that.

I actually always encouraged a bit of cowboyism in the Army. I reasoned that if a guy is being a cowboy, thinking, aren't I cool, aren't I great, look at the smock, he can't then suddenly turn round and start complaining when it begins to rain and he's stuck in a trench. Hardly very outdoor-loving and macho that, is it? No, if you're a cowboy, then you can't complain. I was as frustrated as hell about those Northern Ireland boots though. Of course, I know now they were completely right to cut them off. They couldn't mess around. But at times like that, one's brain works in an irrational way, and little things get blown up out of all proportion.

When they cut off my smock, however, a grenade fell out of it and hit the ground. There was a bit of panic and a scuffle, but the pin was still in. I think I found it all vaguely amusing. Then I remember they found the Colt 45. One of the orderlies handed it to somebody else who said, 'It's loaded but it's not made ready.' And for some ridiculous reason, I felt reassured by that. It made me think he knew what he was doing, even though it wasn't arms he was meant to know how to deal with but my injury.

I asked them where they were going to put the pistol, because I wanted it so much, and they said I would get it back later. But I never did. Even with this gigantic hole in my head, I could be worried about things like that.

They operated on me a while afterwards, stopping the blood loss and removing the obvious dead tissue and various bits of dirt and muck. Then they packed the wound full of antiseptic gel, and stretched my scalp back over the hole. A piece of skull about four and a half by three and a half inches had gone, but the split in the scalp made by the bullet's air turbulence went cleanly back together again.

I think the operation lasted about seven hours in all, and I was conscious through most of it. It did, in fact, seem quite quick, and I was thrilled that someone was finally doing something to help me.

From Fitzroy I was transferred by helicopter to the Red Cross ship the *Uganda*, which was floating in the Falklands Sound and out of bounds to the war. I remember being staggered by the sight of a bed and clean sheets, after all that time in trenches and dirt. Even more shattering was the sight of priests of every denomination gathered like vultures waiting for us to die.

My head still hurt like hell, but they wouldn't let me go into a deep sleep. Every half-hour they brought me round to take my pulse, temperature and blood pressure and shine a pen torch in my eyes to test the reaction of the pupils. When you're as ill as I was, and haven't slept for days previously anyway, all you want to do is sleep, but it was too dangerous. They did not want me to go into a deep sleep in case I died. And I lay there thinking that I was undergoing the sort of sensory deprivation that forms part of the exercises on an interrogation course. I was being fed by drips, so I couldn't eat or taste anything. I couldn't feel anything because I was paralysed. I couldn't pee, because I had a catheter in, couldn't see anything but the ceiling above, and couldn't hear anything because the ship was being kept so quiet.

By now, I was desperately keen to know when I was going to go back home to England. Forty-eight times a day I must have asked people, is it the next day yet, is it time to go?

Eventually Angus Smith, our padre, came to visit us, and told me that the war was over. I had mixed reactions then. I was pleased that my boys would not have to go and fight any more battles. But I also wondered why there were no other platoon commanders lying in the ward. If they had been doing their job, leading from the front, should there not have been more of them here, with me, in intensive care? Where the hell were they all?

It is a reaction I shall probably come under criticism for, but it was honestly what I thought then. Looking back, of course, I realize that I was being very unfair; a lot of platoon commanders were lying injured in other wards, and a number of others had been killed.

I don't think that at that point I really had any comprehension of how ill I actually was. I know that I used to have nightmares on the *Uganda*, and that one night I woke up in the middle of one and grabbed a nurse by the throat. I was generally in a lot of pain, extremely uncomfortable and feeling very sorry for myself, and I desperately wanted to go home. I missed my family, and I was terribly worried about them. I also felt extremely envious of the people who were still on the Falklands — those who had been there for the surrender. I felt that I had missed out on all the fun. They would be there now, running around with all the Argentinian equipment. The victors. It would have been like Christmas, and I really envied them that. I couldn't be one of them any more and couldn't be treated the same. That's what I felt at that point on the *Uganda*. I did not realize then that this was merely a foretaste of how things were going to be again and again, in the years to come.

* * *

After about five days on the *Uganda*, I was transferred to the *Herald*; it was a warship but was being used as a hospital ship, running a taxi service to Montevideo, in Uruguay, from where the injured would be flown home. At this stage, although I was still on the danger list, I was feeling slightly better. On the *Uganda*, just before I left, a young nurse had given me my first bit of physiotherapy. He obviously thought I was going to be paralysed for a long time and quite rightly decided that I should be making an early start, even though I could do none of the exercises he asked me to do at the time.

On the *Herald*, I felt very excited about the prospect of going home. The ship appeared to have been gutted to make one large ward, which had rows and rows of three-tier bunk beds; the staff were mainly volunteers from the naval ratings, plus a couple of doctors and some medics for emergencies.

We were a mixed bunch on board; some were far more ill than others. Many sat around chatting, reading magazines and watching videos. At one point they put on Sam Peckinpah's *Cross of Iron*, which panicked and upset quite a lot of people, and wasn't, perhaps, the most apt of films in the circumstances.

In the main, though, morale was high, because we were going home. The atmosphere was fairly relaxed, too, and I was allowed, at last, to smoke. I remember how great it was when two crew members, who were extremely kind and sympathetic, carried me out on to the helicopter deck at the back of the ship and propped me up in a chair for some fresh air and a cigarette. It was freezing, but I loved it after all those days inside.

I would still wake up in the middle of the night having nightmares, at which point a naval rating on duty would come over and join me for a cigarette, a coffee or a beer — all the things you should not have when you are really ill. But there were times when it was just the sort of thing most of us wanted, and we needed someone to sit and talk to us and stop us from feeling afraid.

One night a paratrooper in the bed behind me, a really loud-mouthed Tom who was very funny and a sort of barrack-room lawyer to boot, suddenly asked me for my officer's issue watch. 'You won't need it,' he said, 'because even if you don't die, you're certainly going to be out of the Army. And no one will ever miss it.' I let him have it. He seemed to have a point at the time. Years later I remember seeing him again at some church service. He still had the watch.

Infection was a big danger while I was on the *Herald*, and I needed constant injections of antibiotics to keep it at bay. They couldn't keep puncturing my arm, as it would soon have been as buggered-up as a heroin addict's. Instead they inserted what looked like a horse needle into a vein. It had a plastic cap on the top of it, which I used to call the manhole cover, and every so often they could attach a new syringe to it. It was quite a palaver getting this huge great needle into a vein, and I remember that when the doctor and a medic were standing on a bottom bunk trying to do it for me, suddenly there was this little 'errr...' noise followed by a thud. The medic had passed out, which everyone thought very amusing.

All in all, the *Herald* trip was a happy time. Morale, as I've said, was high. We were all wounded together, but we had won, and we were going home.

'DOWNGRADED TO SERIOUSLY ILL'

John Lawrence

There are jays on Barnes Common, and on Sunday morning, four days after we'd first heard that Robert had been injured, there was one sitting in the tree opposite the house as we left for church. I said thanks under my breath that it was not a magpie and had the usual moral tussle in my mind as I told myself not to be superstitious. As we crossed the common two magpies flew over us, so that was all right. Robert was prayed for in the intercession and I later found out that he was prayed for in forty churches that day from Anglican in Sydney to Presbyterian in Edinburgh and from Dutch Reform in Cape Town to Roman Catholic in London. A young lecturer at Jean's college paid to have a Mass said for him in Westminster Cathedral, and a back-door pavilion steward at Lord's paid to have one said in his Catholic church in Brentford. This news gave us great courage and comfort.

After church that first Sunday, we got home to find Kim Ross waiting. He had been Robert's second-in-command in Northern Ireland and had served with Chris in Germany. Now he was personal staff officer to the GOC Northern Ireland and he had come across for the weekend after hearing about Robert.

Kim, as always, was cheerful and ebullient. Putney Fair was under way at the other end of the common and I was dreading his suggesting we go to it. Instead, he suggested we go out to lunch. A new restaurant had just opened on the Lower Richmond Road. The meal was passable and the wine reasonable, but I could not stand that false cheerfulness.

How could I think that? After all, when Robert had first gone to war I had prayed that he be given strength, courage and cheerfulness. The answer was that I had long since changed my prayer to 'God give him strength and courage and hope'.

Kim could see I was restless and suggested we walk home while the others had more coffee. I was off like a shot. When we got in, Kim rang the duty clerk at Headquarters Scots Guards. There had been another signal. 'Downgraded to seriously ill and transferred to hospital ship *Herald*.' We both leapt with joy and pranced around the drawing room wishing the others would get home to share the news. I fetched my bagpipes from upstairs and struck up. Tuning was hardly necessary as I played up and down the room — Scotland the Brave, Tiree Love Song, Morag of Dunvegan, Heroes of Kohima, High Road to Linton.

Kim sat grinning and when I finished, exhausted, he applauded. 'I bet you've never played better, John.' He was very kind because I am strictly a self-taught, play-by-ear, tinker-piper. To inflict myself on a lieutenant-colonel in the Scots Guards was a bit naughty. The others came home and we opened another bottle.

* * *

On the Monday morning, one week exactly after Robert was shot, I spoke again with the Lieutenant Colonel Commanding. He had managed a short, garbled conversation with the battalion Commanding Officer over the radio and had gathered that Robert could speak; that his speech was slurred, but he was making sense. I thanked him for this morsel of information and telephoned home.

There was no more news until about midnight on Tuesday night, when the telephone rang. I leapt out of bed to answer it.

'This is wireless station Portishead. I have warship *Herald* for you,' the operator said.

A series of pips followed and then a voice came crackling through, impatient with the quality of the connection.

'Hello, hello, HELLO!'

'Robert, is that you?'

Jean jumped from the bed and was beside me in a flash.

'Daddy? Have they told you what they've done to me?'

'Well, a bit, but you tell me.'

'They've shot the top of my bloody head off. We're due at Brize Norton on Friday, can you be there?'

'Of course we'll be there.'

'But it'll be half-past five in the morning.'

'I don't care when it is, we'll be there. Here's your Mummy.'

Jean took the phone and through her tears told him we loved him, then had to hand it back. I tried to encourage him and then the operator interrupted.

'I'm afraid this call must now be terminated.'

THE JOURNEY HOME

Robert Lawrence

My first phone call home to my parents was incredible. Very emotional. After I'd spoken to Daddy and my mother came on the extension, we all started crying. And I remember feeling a terrible sense of desolation when I asked them to come and meet me at Brize Norton — a feeling that they might not be able to make it. In some way I had regressed into childhood again, and was dreadfully afraid that they wouldn't turn up. But Daddy said something reassuring along the lines of, 'You try and stop us, we'll be there.' And then this cold operator's voice just suddenly broke in and terminated the call.

I was carried back to my bed in tears, thinking to myself, I wish to God I'd never made that call.

The next big depression and panic occurred shortly after this when I was told that, once I got to Montevideo, I would have to go to a neurological hospital there for a brain scan. If this showed up any air bubbles or other complications associated with the brain, then I would not be allowed to go home, because the flight back to England would kill me. The idea of being stuck in a South American hospital, in a country bang next door to the one we had just been fighting, with none of my relatives and friends around to visit me, was terrifying. On top of this, there was a rumour going around that special Argentinian hit squads had been sent out to Montevideo to get the British wounded. God knows how true that was, but the staggering thing was that at the time I believed it. It hardly helped matters.

We had an armed police escort in our ambulance car through Montevideo, together with police escorts on bikes and in cars, their American-type sirens going full blast. The police were all carrying guns in holsters. It was bizarre; they looked almost identical to the Argentinians we had just been fighting — same faces, same uniforms, everything.

One of them asked me, in broken English, whether I spoke Spanish. All I could come up with were things like, 'hands up', 'surrender' and 'where is your officer?' — all the helpful little phrases we had been taught on the way down to the Falklands on the QE2. It was all quite a joke by then.

The brain scan was excruciatingly painful. They injected me with a chemical dye that circulated in the bloodstream to show up any abnormalities. The pain in my head was already agonizing, and this just piled on more pain. There was a burning sensation in my head and a needle stuck into my arm. It was at this point that I began to realize that this was just the beginning. It dawned on me that I would go through months and months of being hurt by people from then on. And I was right.

* * *

Having checked my brain scan, the doctors thankfully decided that I was fit to fly, and I was taken off to an airport and put on board an RAF VC10 medical air ambulance. It was an enormous plane with stretchers in the sides. I had a bottom stretcher 'bunk' and, because my left arm was paralysed and totally limp, it kept dropping down out of the bed and on to the floor. The Air Force steward kept stepping on it. Of course, I couldn't feel anything and it became quite a joke, really; I used to pull his leg about it.

At one stage, I remember being brought one of those classic aircraft meals, with everything in separate little plastic compartments. I was eating it off the floor, my bad arm across me, when I spotted some black goo-like stuff in one of the plastic containers. What's this? I wondered. I was about to give it a try, when I realized that the goo had in fact been dripping down on to the tray from my head. It was blood and cerebral fluid, oozing out because of the air pressure, which was doing me quite a lot of damage.

It was a very painful journey. But by then, I seemed always to be in pain, so I hardly noticed the extra extremes. When we finally landed at Brize Norton, after a flight of about seventeen hours, I just remember feeling thrilled to be back in England — even if it was, as usual, pouring with rain.

An Air Force officer came aboard, soon after we'd landed, and said to me, 'Your parents are here. But they'll be meeting you later at RAF Wroughton.'

This upset me tremendously, and I said, 'Why there? Why not here?'

'Because,' he replied, 'no one's being allowed to stay here.'

All family and all press were banned from meeting us at Brize Norton, I learned only later, because it appears they didn't want the severely injured people, the really badly burned and maimed young men, to be seen. The press had, however, been allowed to take pictures earlier at Brize Norton of a group of the walking wounded, who had returned home with a scar on the cheek, perhaps, or an arm in a sling or a slight limp or a couple of crutches. These, apparently, represented the agreeable image of wounded heroes, whereas we were cut off from view before being loaded, under cover, as it were, on to buses. I was amazed and horrified. I had honestly thought that there would be some sort of reception committee at Brize Norton for us. I'd thought we were going to be treated like heroes. Having been naked on the *Herald*, in my stretcher bed, I'd even gone around desperately trying to find some uniform to wear for the welcome home. All I'd managed in the end were a tatty old pair of combat trousers and a naval rating's shirt. But I'd wanted to come off that plane as a soldier — a heroic soldier, what's more, who had just helped win a war. I was still pretty naïve then, I suppose, and was only just beginning to get an insight into this whole business of the Government's control over the images of the Falklands War — which ones should be seen and which ones needed to be contained.

I distinctly remember having quite an argument with the nurse on the way to Wroughton about the fact that I didn't want to be carted off to another bloody hospital after having travelled eight and a half thousand miles from the Falklands. I just wanted to go home. I had no comprehension then of how very near to death I was. The fact was, I had travelled very badly and apparently a lot of the people who had been with me thought that if I didn't die during the trip, then I would soon after.

REUNION

John Lawrence

On Thursday, Headquarters Scots Guards telephoned to confirm the expected time of arrival of the flight from Montevideo.

Robert's girlfriend Mitty came with us, which was very brave of her, though she was a bit shattered when we arrived at Brize Norton guardroom to find an ex-girlfriend going through just before us.

Inside the terminal building, which I knew well, I went to the passenger desk to enquire about the flight. The young corporal was pleasant, but busy, and did not have time to check the Montevideo manifest in the middle of getting a draft off to Hong Kong as well as preparing to receive a flight from Akrotiri which had been delayed three hours.

A young WRAF officer appeared on the scene and I collared her with my questions. There were others asking as well. A Welsh couple in particular were very upset. They had been at Brize Norton for a day and a half hoping to meet their son. He had been badly burned but that was all they knew. When they had met the flight the day before, he had not been on it as expected and now they were frantic and near to desperation. They had been given overnight accommodation. 'Very comfortable, but we'd rather he'd been on the proper flight,' said the little Welsh lady, her eyes full of tears.

A squadron leader came out to see what the problem was. I could not believe my luck. It was Norman Haggett, with whom I had played a lot of RAF cricket. He had always been a dour bat, rather in the Boycott mould,

capable of brilliant shots, but more often than not content
slowly to accumulate the runs.

He was equally surprised to see me, but the superficial
bonhomie of exchanging greetings which is so much a
part of service life soon passed when I told him why I
was there. He disappeared again and came back after
ten minutes with the latest ETA from Montevideo and a
list of passengers. Robert was on it and so was the Welsh
Guardsman.

'Any chance of my coming out to the aircraft, Norman?'
I asked.

'I doubt it very much, but I'll see what I can do.'

We waited impatiently. The newsagent opened, but I
was not interested in the news, though I bought a paper
to get change for the coffee machine. The brown liquid it
produced was awful, just like airline coffee with powdered
milk and too hot to drink.

At last an excited buzz went through the building and
we learned that the Montevideo casualty evacuation flight
had landed. I searched for Norman and spotted his red
duty movements officer's armband. He saw me coming
and shrugged his shoulders, then disappeared. 'You'll not
run me out today, Haggett,' I muttered, the frustration
and anticipation building up inside me.

He reappeared after five minutes and this time came
straight towards us. No one would be allowed to see
the passengers at Brize Norton. They would be taken to
Princess Alexandra's RAF hospital at Wroughton where
a proper reception centre had been set up. I protested
strongly, but Norman was adamant. He seemed embarrassed that he could not be of more help. I asked if he
had seen Robert. He said he had and had told him we
were here and would see him at Wroughton. That at
least was something, but he would tell us no more. Jean,
Mitty and I went back to the car, deflated, worried and a
little angry. It was still pouring with rain. The ex-girlfriend
caught me in the car-park and asked what was happening.
The poor soul looked utterly bewildered when I told

her and tried to explain the twenty-six-mile route to Wroughton.

When we got to the hospital I went straight to the Commanding Officer's office. It was a large hospital and three of us — Jean, Nick and I — had been patients there at various times. I had not met the Air Commodore before, but his Air Officer Commanding at Support Command had been a cadet with me and we had remained friends for over thirty years. He had telephoned me the day before and said that he had spoken with the CO at Wroughton, asking him to look after us.

The CO was a nice man and took us straight down to the reception area. His wife was there organizing tea and coffee for the waiting families. The whole place had the atmosphere of a village hall receiving flood victims.

Two Scots Guards senior non-commissioned officers came up to us and saluted. I knew them both and Jean knew one. The drill sergeant had been Christopher's platoon sergeant in Germany when he had commanded the mortar platoon. The other one was the colour sergeant from the orderly room. The ex-girlfriend appeared and Jean explained to the drill sergeant that Robert must not be upset by her being there. A bit later the poor girl left in tears. I felt awful about it, but then the Air Commodore appeared again.

'John,' he said, 'I'll just show you where Ward 10 is. It's where Robert will be when they transfer him from the ambulance.'

I followed him out into the corridor, leaving Jean and Mitty talking with the two sergeants.

'Look, that's Ward 10, the next corridor on the right, but that's not why I've called you out. The sisters are a bit worried about Robert. He's had a bad journey and is still seeping brain fluid from the wound. If he leaves you when you're in seeing him, grab your wife, won't you.'

I nodded and thanked him but the words had not sunk

in. Only afterwards did I realize he was telling me Robert might well die.

We went slowly up the corridor, Jean holding my hand, Mitty following behind. The ward was full and there were screens round some of the beds. Robert was in the first bed on the left. The shock of seeing him was unnerving. I stood rooted to the spot while his mother went round the bed to his left-hand side. She bent to kiss him, recoiling momentarily from the black, weeping wound, nine inches long, that began just three inches above his right eye and disappeared over the top of his head. He turned his head to her and reached out with his right hand.

'Hello, Mummy,' he said, muffled by her embrace and by the tears that welled up in his eyes.

Jean straightened up and let Mitty in to kiss him gently on the lips. She was only nineteen, but very brave as she fought back the tears.

I stepped forward and Robert turned his head towards me, revealing a dark stain on the pillow. From the wound, black lumps protruded between the stitch marks. Later I learned they were actually parts of his brain. He managed a weak smile as I took his right hand and bent to kiss his forehead.

'Oh, Daddy, I'm sorry, it wasn't worth it.'

My heart sank. If he had gone through all this and thought it was not worth it, then we were in real trouble. He was a soldier, serving his Queen and country, just as his brother, his father, his grandfathers, his two great-uncles and even his mother had done. 'Not worth it' was almost unacceptable, yet this was what Robert, lying wounded, was saying. He had every right if that was what he really thought.

In my pocket I had a full list of Scots Guards casualties which for some reason the Lieutenant Colonel Commanding had given me. I remembered some of the names: Warrant Officer II Wight, the six-foot-eight drill sergeant who had been on the Ceremony of the Keys with Robert, and Guardsman Tanbini who had been in Christopher's platoon in Germany, both dead; McEntaggart and Pengelly, both in Robert's No. 3 platoon and both wounded.

Robert's grip in his right hand was like iron, just as it had been when I had said goodbye nearly seven weeks before. I was confused as I kissed his forehead and wondered if he really did feel it had not been worth it.

'Don't say that, Spud. You've been so brave and it'll come right, I'm sure.'

'But, Daddy, it was not worth it. I've lost all my men.'

'No you haven't. There are nine dead, Robert, but none from No. 3 Platoon.'

'What about Sergeant Jackson? What about McEntaggart and Morton and Pengelly? They're all dead, and because of me.'

'Robert, they are not. The Lieutenant Colonel Commanding has given me a full casualty list. Look, I've got it here. Sergeant Jackson is not on it. McEntaggart and Morton are wounded, but they'll be all right. OK, Pengelly is seriously ill, but he'll come through it. He's one of your boys so he's bound to come through.'

Robert began to calm down a little. A sister appeared and asked us to leave because the doctors were coming to see the patients. He waved and smiled weakly as we left.

Outside, Jean cried softly and asked me if I thought he would be all right. I tried to comfort her, and Mitty too, arguing that he had been upset because he thought he'd lost all his men. Under provisions of the Geneva Convention, fighting troops cannot go on hospital ships, so once Robert had been transferred to the *Uganda* and the *Herald* he would have been cut off from the battalion and would not have known its fate. When I saw his Commanding Officer weeks later, he explained that Robert's men had suffered the same lack of information. Many of them thought Robert was dead before he left the island and all thought he would never get home alive.

The two sergeants greeted us back in the reception area and one of them fetched Jean and Mitty a cup of coffee. Within ten minutes we were invited back to the ward and we asked them to come with us. At first they were reluctant, but Jean persuaded them. It was exactly the right thing to do. As we came through the door and Robert saw the chequered hat bands, the gleaming cap stars, the red and blue stable belts, he beamed, a totally different person from the one we had left.

Without ostentation, but immaculately, both sergeants stopped at the bottom of the bed, ramrod straight, and saluted in unison. Then, moving forward in turn, the drill sergeant first, they each shook his one good hand and greeted him. Beneath the formality of these senior non-commissioned officers, their genuine respect for the young wounded officer burned through and I felt very proud.

Nurses arrived with a wheeled stretcher and lifted Robert off the bed. I was surprised when they pulled back the bedclothes and his left leg moved a little, but I soon realized it had been only an involuntary twitch. It was a struggle getting Robert on to the stretcher but eventually he was on and was then wheeled away. He was to be taken to the Queen Elizabeth Hospital, Woolwich, and then to the Maudsley Hospital in South London the next morning for an operation on the wound.

As we drove away we passed the helipad and stopped to watch the big Chinook being loaded with patients. We could pick out the burns cases because of the bandages but we were too far away to spot Robert. From the aircrew mess behind us the crew appeared in their flying overalls, carrying their 'bone-domes' under their arms. I recognized the pilot, Squadron Leader Dick Forsythe. We had been together at Odiham when he was first on 72 Squadron. I wound down the window.

'Hello, sir,' he said. 'What are you doing here?'

'I'm just making sure you fly that thing properly, Dick. You've got my youngest son on board.'

'Right, sir, don't you worry. We're dropping a few off at Halton and then on to Woolwich.'

He waved, and ten minutes later the great twin-rotored helicopter lumbered into the air and then, nose down, flew off at surprising speed.

We set off on the long drive back to London. To begin with, nothing was said. Then Jean started to ask her questions out loud.

'Will he be all right? Will the operation be a success? What exactly have they got to do? Where are they going to do it?'

'The Maudsley.' I should not have tried to answer.

'Where's that?'

'I don't know. Denmark Hill I think.'

'Who is the surgeon?'

'I forget his name, Peter something, I think, but he's brilliant, they say, and he's flying back from holiday in South Africa tonight especially to operate on Robert.'

'Surely not.'

'That's what the Air Commodore told me.' I tried to break the sequence. 'Funny about air commodores.'

'What's funny about air commodores?'

'Their badge of rank is one thick ring. Dick Forsythe's father is one and he was President of the London Irish Rugby Club. I was proposing the guests at a dinner once when he and Bob Weighill were there and I explained that wing commanders had three rings and air commodores like Bob had one thick one, but Paddy Forsythe being Irish had an even thicker one.'

It did not get much of a laugh from Jean but it did stop the questions. Mitty was asleep in the back.

The rain started again and I had to concentrate hard as we sped up the crowded M4. Neither of us spoke very much. We just wanted to get home to tell the other boys, and, of course, Melanie.

That evening Chris and Nick went to Woolwich to see Robert. They called in on the way home and confirmed the arrangements for the operation the next morning.

The two boys were clearly very shaken by their visit to Robert, and Nick was angry about some doctor at

Woolwich who had upset him with some petty regulation requirement. Chris had apparently done his Adjutant 1st Battalion act and had put him down with some non-combatant taunt. I suggested quietly that in fact doctors, even Army doctors, were very important right now.

THE MAUDSLEY
HOSPITAL

Robert Lawrence

Not long after I arrived at the Queen Elizabeth Hospital, I remember dozing in my bed in the intensive care ward and then suddenly seeing a group of Army doctors at the end of it, discussing my notes. One of them said something like, 'I wonder what kind of bullet hit him?'

I said, 'A Belgian FN 7.62.'

'Hmm,' they went, and carried on chatting among themselves. Then another one piped up, 'Anyone know the muzzle velocity of an FN 7.62?'

'Three thousand eight hundred feet per second,' I said. 'Why don't you ask me if you want to know?'

I was told to calm down and reminded that I was still under Queen's Regulations. I didn't give a damn about Queen's Regulations at that moment. I was pretty stroppy, and I told the doctor in question that he could shove his Queen's Regulations. And his rank. Disillusionment, together with all the frustrations and pain of the last ten days, were beginning to have their effect.

My brothers, Chris and Nick, and Nick's wife, Melanie, came to visit me at Woolwich. I remember Chris finding it all very difficult and upsetting which seemed odd to me then, because he was a soldier himself. By the same token, it seemed odd to me that Nick was taking it so much better, and being so strong, when he had never had anything to do with the Army. All the time I was chatting to them, I was thinking, 'God, this is so strange, Chris being so upset, and him a soldier.' But of course I realize now that that's precisely *why* he was so much more upset. He had been a soldier, and I had

62

ROBERT LAWRENCE

been a soldier after him. Now this had happened. He
probably felt — even though he should not have — a bit
responsible.

Then Melanie passed out at the sight of my head.
I imagine there must have been a lot of goo on my
pillow. That upset me. But later on I was even more
upset when they let me watch television. It was the
evening of 25 June, and the news was all about the IRA
Hyde Park bombing, killing troops and horses from the
Household Cavalry. A colleague of mine, Anthony Daly,
had been among those killed, leaving behind a widow. They
had been married for less than a month.

I was disgusted and desperately upset, because I thought
I had left all this behind. I had left a war to come back to
good old England and now, as soon as I was back, a friend
gets blown up just down the road and I have to watch all
the graphic details about it on the television news. I got
extremely upset with the nurse for letting me see it. She
must have known that coverage of the bombing would
have been appearing on television. Eventually I ended up
having a hell of an argument with her, even to the point of
asking her her commission date in order that I could pull
rank. Of course, I know now it was all a bit unfair. There
is no rank in hospital anyway.

A lot of things I did and said then might now, five
years later, seem quite unjustified. But one has to try and
understand what happens to the mind of a young man who
has been taught by the Army to have pride in himself,
pride in being able to look after himself, and then suddenly
finds himself injured and dependent on everyone else. His
reactions might seem illogical or unjust. His priorities
might seem wildly out of proportion. There is frustration
and fear, and there is a wounded pride to go with the
wounded body. The upshot of it all is that the smallest
things seem, at the time, all-important and provoke big
reactions.

* * *

After one night at the Queen Elizabeth Hospital I was transferred to the Maudsley in Camberwell, South London. Apart from remembering vaguely that the nurse who went with me was very attractive, I cannot recall much about the journey, because I had been given a pre-med before I left.

I was to go to the Maudsley for major neuro-surgery which lasted, I was later told, about six hours. The surgeon initially opened up two of the stitches that had been holding my scalp together, and my head apparently just burst open with rotten matter. He cut away the dead and obviously infected tissue of the brain and then removed deep bits of dirt that had been dragged in by the bullet and its subsequent air vacuum. A scan had also revealed that a piece of the beret I'd been wearing was right in the centre of my brain, and had to be removed.

Following this, the surgeon cut open my right thigh to remove a piece of muscle sheath. He used a patch of this strong material to cover the hole where my skull had been blown away, and then sewed my scalp back together again. I didn't know it at the time, obviously, but during this operation and the initial stages of my recovery, the Queen had asked for regular updates on my progress. She had expressed her concern about the war earlier when she had met my father at Lords.

When I came round from the operation, I saw an old man in the bed opposite who had also just been operated on. I believe he had a fractured skull. They tried to give him water, but he just kept vomiting. He could not, after the anaesthetic, hold it down. I was absolutely starving, though, because I had not been given anything to eat for about thirty hours. There had been drips over the past few days, but I could not recall having eaten anything by mouth since the flight home. I was demanding food, and the staff insisted that I would not be able to keep it down. But in the end, after about a twenty-minute argument with Mary, an old Irish nurse, I was presented with egg and chips, which I duly ate, and then asked for more. And I ate that as well.

John Lawrence

Robert's operation took place at ten o'clock in the morning and we were told to ring at teatime, say about half-past four. It was the longest day I can remember, but at last the time came and I rang the Maudsley Hospital. They told me all seemed to be well though Robert was not really conscious yet. I rang again two hours later to be told he was sitting up in bed eating egg and chips. It never occurred to me that he would probably have to be spoon fed or at the very least have it all cut up for him. We were told we could see him the next day and we could also see the surgeon.

The only parking space was marked 'Doctor' but I took it. After all, I was going to see my son who had been shot in the Falklands. We followed the signs to the ward and were met by a rather bossy sister who explained that Robert would have to behave himself because there were some very sick patients in the ward. It was the intensive care ward and they had nowhere else to put him. I suggested he was not too well himself and she agreed, conceding that what she had meant was that he could not be in a ward on his own.

His head was swathed in bandages. Jean pointed out that that was better than our being able to see the awful wound. She had been really shocked by that the day before.

The patient in the next bed groaned and Robert explained that they were all cases in which the brain had been affected, either by fractures or by brain tumours. Obviously he was depressed by them all. He longed for a cigarette but had been forbidden to smoke because of the oxygen cylinders in the room. He reached across to his locker and I went straight to help him.

'It's all right, Daddy, I can do it.'

He struggled to reach the beaker of orange squash.

'It's difficult, but I've got to do it,' he said. 'The trouble is my balance. I fell out of bed last night.'

I could not believe it and was all for complaining, but Jean restrained me.

The surgeon was a pleasant man, about my age. He began to explain what had been involved in the operation.

At Montevideo the surgeons had done a brain scan which he offered to show us. He switched on a viewing screen behind him and the dark shadow of a skull appeared. There was a muzzy patch on the right side and about half a dozen bright spots of varying size scattered over that same side. He explained that these were bits of bone and beret which had been driven into the brain by the impact of the bullet. One was particularly deep and had taken a lot of getting out. They had done a marvellous job in the field hospital, but inevitably some infection had developed in the twelve days since Robert had been shot. He explained that when he had opened up the wound it had virtually erupted in a heaving mass. I thought I was going to be sick and I squeezed Jean's hand under the table.

The surgeon went on, quietly and without fuss. A lot of brain material had been removed by the high-velocity bullet which, apart from penetrating the skull, travels so fast that it sets up a shock wave around it which removes anything in its way as effectively as the bullet itself. This, plus the necessity to remove the infection, meant that Robert had lost about forty-five per cent of his brain material, including the whole of the motor area for the left-hand side of the body.

Jean and I looked at each other and then almost in unison asked if Robert would ever get back the use of his arm.

'I doubt it very much, although it is just possible that other parts of the brain may take over and give him some facility maybe to hold something against his body. You'd be surprised how well people adapt to having only one limb, be it one arm or one leg.'

That prompted the next question and again we both asked together, 'How about walking? Will he be in a wheelchair all his life?'

'To some extent that will depend on him, but if he does manage to walk it will always be with a very severe limp.'

He told us there was a danger of epilepsy, and Robert would have to take phenotone pills to reduce the risk of attacks, but by far the biggest worry was whether all the infection had been removed. There had been so much and the surgeon was afraid he might not have removed quite all the infected material before patching the six-by-two hole in the dura with a piece of thigh muscle.

He made the whole business sound like paring a rotten apple to cut away all the brown bits. As for the dura, I had to look that up — the bag-like membrane inside the skull that contains the brain.

The surgeon switched off the screen and stood up with his hand outstretched. I took it and thanked him for saving Robert's life. He shrugged it off modestly and explained that he had said before going on holiday to South Africa that he would come straight back if any Falklands cases came up.

We went back to the ward to say goodbye to Robert. For that we had to be cheerful and full of hope and I found it nigh on impossible.

When we visited the next day I was amazed to find that Robert was not in his bed. We found him in a wheelchair round the corner and down the corridor talking to two very large gentlemen and, inevitably, smoking a cigarette. The Lieutenant Colonel Commanding greeted me and I introduced him to Jean. In turn he introduced us to Desmond Langley, the General Officer Commanding Household Division.

They both made kind noises about how brave Robert had been. In particular they were both very impressed by how clearly he could remember the battle. This was extremely interesting and very useful.

When they had gone I asked Robert if he really could remember the battle.

'Oh yes,' he said, 'I never lost consciousness. When they were carrying me down the mountain I could hear them saying, "Mr Lawrence is deid, the bastards have killed Mr Lawrence" and I couldn't tell them I was not bloody deid. It was only when we got to the bottom and they laid me down that I managed to move and they realized I was alive.'

He went on to tell us how Sammy Drennan had flown him out, against orders, and how he had shouted for attention at the Field Hospital in Fitzroy.

'The next thing I knew I was in a bed on the *Uganda* hospital ship surrounded by priests. I told the RC in no uncertain terms I was no Tague; in fact, I told them all they could clear off because I was not going to die yet, thank you very much!'

I was surprised how easily he could talk about it. It was almost as if he enjoyed it, as though the excitement was a drug which lifted and animated him. Tears were never far from my eyes as I listened and I found it hard to believe that this pale broken body lying in front of us, the fruit of our love for each other, had been through so much.

'That's enough, Spud,' I said, 'I think you should get some rest.'

The bossy sister appeared with the same message and began to wheel him back to the ward.

'He's had eight visitors today, before you came,' she said. 'It's too many and, besides, it upsets the rest of the ward. That's why he's out here in the corridor, that and his insistence on smoking. I tell you, he's more trouble than the rest put together.'

I looked at her and she knew I was angry, but when I spoke I did not raise my voice.

'I don't give a damn how much trouble he is to you, Sister. All I know is he's been through more trouble than you'll ever know. Robert has been wounded fighting for his country, for the likes of you and me. He's not just some routine patient to obey your pettifogging regulations. He and others like him have been through hell and he does not deserve to come to a place like this to be bossed around by a misery-guts like you.'

She stormed out and a nurse came in to take the wheelchair and Robert back to his bed. She smiled and winked at me as she went past and I wished I had not been so rude to the sister.

'Don't worry, Daddy, I'll be all right,' said Robert.

Jean and I kissed him and left. She took my hand and squeezed it, but said nothing on the way to the car. As we drove home I wondered how many people in the other cars on the road had had anything at all to do with the war in the Falklands apart from seeing it on the television or in the newspapers.

Robert Lawrence

The Maudsley, I thought, was old-fashioned and grim. I hated it. Most people in my ward seemed to be in a coma, and the night staff did not seem to be either well-trained or particularly interested. Since then, the staff have all changed. But while I was there I remember in particular two night nurses who looked as if they were capable of no more than pushing a button if something went wrong.

Once, when they were having a conversation and I was feeling really lonely, needing to talk to someone, I heard one say she was pregnant. So, trying to be chatty, I asked her when the baby was due. She got quite ratty with me, and told me to mind my own business and not to listen to other people's conversations. The insensitivity upset me dramatically at the time.

Once, in the ward, I remember picking up a cigarette-lighter which had been in my locker and attempting to set fire to my left hand. I had got this bizarre idea into my head that if I attempted to set fire to it and hurt it, it would come back to life. The staff were very irate about that — rightly so, of course. There was a rumpus, too, when I fell out of bed. After managing to get myself sitting up, I leaned slightly across the bed, but my left buttock couldn't save me, and I ended up landing on my head on the floor. The nicer part about it was that later they sent a really kind doctor to sort out the fuss and he ended up bringing me a beer and having a chat.

I was determined to be allowed to smoke. In the ward, of course, the oxygen cylinders represented a fire hazard. The staff also said smoking would be harmful to my lungs after anaesthetic. Finally, they said I would be allowed to smoke the next day. So at 5.30 a.m. the following morning I got them to push my bed out into the corridor and then lit up.

An enormous number of friends visited me at the Maudsley. For some bizarre reason, the girls would all bring me copies of *Playboy* magazine, which they seemed to think was the thing to do. One day a bunch of friends also got me into a wheelchair and pushed me out into the Maudsley's rose garden.

There I was, sipping champagne and eating strawberries with them when my neuro-surgeon found me. He was absolutely furious. After all, I was still supposed to be in intensive care. So he promptly kicked all my guests out and pushed me back to bed.

After any kind of brain surgery, there is a tendency to suffer clinical depression, and I had some pretty black periods at the Maudsley, some really, really depressing times. I would lie in bed moping, not talking to anybody, which was incredibly difficult for my family to cope with. Each time they arrived, they would get me into a wheelchair, push me out of the ward, and then I'd be in tears, crying my eyes out. My sister-in-law's brother, Gavin, came to see me during one of these black spells, and I was suddenly hit by an overwhelming desire to go to the lavatory, which hardly ever happened, given the way my body was screwed up. Gavin decided against the commode, which they usually just stuffed in front of everyone, and I anyway wanted to go to a proper toilet. So Gavin put me in a wheelchair and took me there. Once we got there, we both cried our eyes out the whole way through. We were struck, I think, by the bloody pathos of it all. It was such a pathetic, unpleasant and sad, sad business.

My first session of physio at the Maudsley also proved to be a horrific business. Two physiotherapists, relatively young girls, put me on a solid bench bed and attempted to teach me to sit up. Owing to the paralysis, however, I just kept collapsing on the left-hand side. Then they dragged in this six-foot mirror. They said they would put it in front of me so that I could see what should happen, even if I could not feel it. What they did not realize was that probably the last time I had looked in a mirror was on the *QE2* on the way down to the Falklands. When I saw my reflection this time, saw what was looking back at me, I absolutely freaked.

I had gone from about twelve and a half stone to just under eight in three weeks, the gash in my head looked grotesque, and my mouth was incessantly dribbling. I reminded myself of charity posters I had seen for the mentally handicapped. Later, I could joke about it to Gavin, but at that first moment, I went berserk, and started to cry and scream.

I turned to the two girl physios and went into this incredibly emotional diatribe about what it is like killing people, and having your friends killed. It was the classic Vietnam syndrome: 'Who the hell are you? You weren't there, you can't know what I'm talking about, you don't know what it's like.'

During this eruption, the hospital chaplain happened to be passing by. He waited until I had completely finished, and then simply said: 'I'm very privileged to have heard that emotional outburst.' I just gaped at him.

WEEKENDS OUT

Robert Lawrence

After a week at the Maudsley, I was transferred back to the Queen Elizabeth Hospital in Woolwich. As an officer, I had a room of my own, off the main ward. It was nice to have privacy again, and I surrounded myself with home comforts — coffee percolator, television, video, the works. I had visits from various dignatories — the Lieutenant Colonel Commanding Scots Guards, for instance, and the Major General Commanding Household Division. The latter brought along Simon Hayward, then his aide-de-camp, with whom I had served in Kenya and who later, in 1987, was imprisoned in Sweden for smuggling drugs.

There were a lot of pleasantries exchanged, and a lot of gassing, especially when the kind of issues came up that I was then really beginning to worry about — a pension and a possible discharge date, for instance. From the time I got on to the *Uganda*, I had realized that I had no future in the Army, and so these matters were crucial to my future. During all those days lying in a hospital bed, what else did I have to think about? But I never seemed to get any really positive response.

In my heart I think I was waiting then, as I have waited for many years since, for some kind of reassurance. I think all I ever wanted was for the Scots Guards to pat me on the back, give me a hug and be *friendly*, be the 'family' they had always claimed to be when I first joined the regiment. I wanted them to ask me if I was all right, and to make some obvious effort to try and help. Instead, I think I just became an embarrassment to them.

For my part, I think owing to my pride, the pride I had in the regiment and the things we had done together, I tried for too long to hide from them what I really felt about my situation. When I met anyone from the Scots Guards and they said, 'Hello, Robert, how are you?' I'd automatically be smiling and saying, 'Very well indeed.' But the fact is that I was not, not at all. Only it took years before I could openly admit it.

There was quite a succession of Army visitors at the QE, and the former Defence Secretary John Nott also came to see me. He just sort of waddled around, I recall, saying what a lovely room I had and what a lot of lovely cards, and then left. I got the feeling he found the whole situation embarrassing as well. When HRH the Duke of Kent, Colonel of the Scots Guards, came to see me, however, he was great. The minute he arrived, he just kicked his whole entourage out of my tiny room, sat on my bed, and had a cup of coffee with me and chatted for about fifteen minutes, with a genuine sense of interest.

All through my stay in Woolwich, I can remember that the thing I always looked forward to most was a weekend at home. I had been allowed a first brief journey to my parents' home in Barnes on the weekend of my twenty-second birthday, on 3 July, in between leaving the Maudsley and going back to the Queen Elizabeth Hospital. My parents had had to make a bed up for me in the drawing room because they couldn't get my wheelchair up the stairs, and at first, I think, no one knew quite how to react. Every time I moved, there was this strange business of the whole family jumping to their feet. If I went to make a cup of coffee or get something, everyone said, 'What can I get you? What do you want?' I ended up telling them all to calm down, but it took a while for them to adjust.

My brother Chris took me out for a walk — or rather a push — around Barnes Common, and started to cry. He just found it so very difficult to accept that his brother was paralysed and in a wheelchair, and his reaction, in turn, upset me a lot. Eventually, we began to watch a cricket match, but after about forty-five seconds, we discovered that another three or four wheelchairs had lined up behind us. It was this business of, if you have a cripple and you spot another, you join up behind him. So this row of wheelchairs emerged, and I couldn't bear it, and had to get away.

During another weekend out, after I had been moved back to Woolwich, Chris and my other brother, Nick, took me to see my girlfriend, Mitty, who lived in Chelsea. It all ended between us that night. I spent an awful night sleeping on a mattress on her floor, knowing that something was wrong, that she had found someone else. And I had a sense that relationships were going to be a lot more worrying in future, and not necessarily in the physical sense. It has always amused me, since I got injured, how the first question a vast cross-section of society would like to ask me is, 'Ho ho ho, can you still get it up, Robert? Can you still have it off?' This wasn't going to be the problem. The problem was going to be finding someone who could understand, and cope with, the demands of my disability. I knew I was stuck with my disability, whether I liked it or not, for the rest of my life. I had no choice. Other people had the choice, however, as to whether or not they could cope with what my disability involved. And if they could not, then often with great regret I would have to shed them. It is something I would always have to worry about.

One weekend, when my parents had gone away to South Africa on holiday, Chris and Nick picked me up and took me home to Barnes. Chris's then girlfriend, Charlotte, who is now his wife, had her car broken into while we were all staying at my parents' house, so we called the police. What happened then might seem unbelievable, but I can promise you that it really did occur.

A big fat copper from the local police station arrived to take down details, and Chris made some quip along the lines of, 'Well, we'll have to tell the local press about this: "Falklands hero's weekend out of hospital smashed by vandals." '

'Who's the hero?' the policeman asked.

And Chris and Nick replied, 'The one in the wheelchair with the shaved head and the bloody great scar.'

After asking what regiment I'd been in, the policeman informed us that he himself had been in one of the parachute regiments — 3 Para, I believe.

'The last time I saw them,' I said, 'they were looking pretty cold and miserable at Bluff Cove.' It seemed a fairly harmless thing to say, but the policeman considered I was somehow being derogatory and we got into a heated exchange. At one point I asked the policeman to stop calling me 'sonny' and start calling me 'sir'. On being asked why, I pointed out that not only did I hold the Queen's Commission, but in uniform he should address all members of the public as such. Removing his cap and placing it on top of Charlotte's car he said to me, 'I'm not in uniform now, sonny, do you want to go round the corner and talk about it?' And there was I, sitting in a wheelchair.

Nick, who doesn't like policemen at the best of times, and who doesn't like the Army much either — it's the uniforms that get to him, I think — had been trying to calm things down; he couldn't believe what was going on. I ended up getting on to my good leg, supporting myself on the guttering of Charlotte's car, and calling the copper a pretty blunt obscenity.

'Right, that's it,' said the policeman. 'I'm arresting you.'

Nick said, 'Well, I'm not going to help you get him into the back of your van,' and I threatened to drag him through every newspaper he could think of. At which point he stormed off.

It was a shocking and horrendous incident, probably one of the worst that was to happen over the next few years. Time and again, for some reason, I seemed to attract this kind of aggro, and still do. I have tried to work out why it is; whether there is an arrogance in my eyes that people don't like, or whether it is just because I'm an easy target. I've been mugged three times since I was shot. What it all boils down to in the end though, I think, is that men are basically aggressive towards other men, and one of the main things that holds them back is the fear of being beaten in any physical conflict. Of course, if the guy opposite them is a hemiplegic, the fear of laying in will be greatly reduced. It's a pretty horrific reflection on modern society and something that my disability made me suddenly vulnerable to.

My parents used to find it hard to believe some of the things that happened to me — and some of the reactions I got from people — in the years after I was injured. They couldn't believe it until they saw it with their own eyes. My mother, for instance, was crossing Harley Street with me one day when an old man shunted me in the back of the legs with a pram and yelled, 'Get a bloody move on, will you!' She was really shocked.

* * *

Back at the Queen Elizabeth Hospital, lying in bed all day, just waiting until the next weekend out, became extremely frustrating. And one day, barely weeks after I had been admitted back there, I decided I was going to escape and see some friends. I knew I could not go back to my own flat near Sloane Square, because I'd be found straightaway. So instead I decided to go and see Hetta, Mitty's sister, who lived near the King's Road.

I bundled a pile of clothes on to my lap in a wheelchair, and spent about an hour getting dressed. One-handedly, I then wheeled myself down the hospital corridor, passing a group of nurses returning from their coffee break on the way.

'Oh, Mr Lawrence,' they giggled, 'are you leaving us?' And I thought determinedly to myself, yes, I bloody well am.

I got to the courtesy phone in the hospital foyer and rang for a taxi. When it arrived, I gave the driver a tenner, and asked him to chuck the wheelchair in the back. I told him they'd let me out for the day and he said, after looking in his rear-view mirror, 'You look as if you've been through the wars, mate.' 'Yes,' I said, 'you're absolutely right.'

After I had been at Hetta's flat for a while, it suddenly struck me that the first thing the hospital would do would be to ring my parents. They would be desperately worried, which seemed unfair, so I decided to telephone my father.

John Lawrence

I walked into my office after lunch one day to find a message on my desk. Would I please ring Robert on 730 4431. I knew it was not the hospital number and asked my secretary if she was sure she had got it right. She assured me she had, but it was not a number either of us knew. When I rang, a girl answered. It was Henrietta, Mitty's sister. 'Oh, hello,' she said, 'I've got Robert with me.'

I could not believe it, but after quite a long pause he came to the telephone.

'Hallo, Daddy.' He sounded upset. 'Look, I'm sorry to give you this trouble, but I was so pissed off with that hospital I just had to get out, so I wheeled myself to reception and used the freefone for a taxi. I am sorry.'

There was no need for him to be sorry and no way I could be angry. I told him so and asked if they knew where he was. He said he had spoken with Chris and he believed he had told them. He was worried because he was supposed to see the neuro-surgeon at five o'clock.

'Don't worry,' I said, 'I'll get you there.'

I left the office and drove to Chelsea. The traffic was appalling, but eventually I found the flat. It was on the first floor and it seems the taxi driver had got Robert into the lift by dragging his wheelchair up the steps to the front hall and had then literally propped him up in the lift. On the first floor the driver had met him, having carried the chair up the stairs. When I got there Robert was sitting in his wheelchair looking absolutely exhausted.

I telephoned Chris. He had not managed to get through to the hospital, so I rang them and spoke to Major Storey, the Queen Alexandra's Royal Army Nursing Corps sister.

'Good afternoon, Major.' I announced myself as calmly as I could. 'I am pleased to tell you I have my son Robert with me.'

'Not half as pleased as I am to hear he is safe,' she said.

I said that I would get him back as soon as I could, but that the traffic was frightful and would she please try and hold the neuro-surgeon until we got there. He was eminent, he was busy, and I was terrified Robert would not see him and we would lose the opportunity of hearing that he was improving, that he was going to get better. Deep down of course I knew he was not going to get better and I just prayed he would get no worse.

Oh God, please give him strength and courage and hope.

It took us nearly two hours to get to Woolwich. Robert slept some of the time, but he did tell me of his 'escape'.

'It's quite difficult to keep these wheelchairs straight with only one hand,' he said. 'There's a tendency to go round in circles. My left foot keeps jumping off too because it's spastic and that's a problem. I keep running over myself.'

I remembered his telling me earlier how his left arm caused him problems too, particularly when he turned over on to it in his sleep. There was no proper feeling in it and he had no idea where it was. Breaking it was therefore a distinct possibility and he had suggested more than once that he'd be better having it amputated. Apart from getting in the way, it was very heavy.

We got to Woolwich at ten past five and waited outside the sister's office. Through the glass we could see the surgeon talking earnestly with an Army doctor. I was relieved to see him still there. Major Storey came out when she saw us and Robert immediately wheeled himself off to the lavatory.

The sister was clearly very upset and I wondered if she had been told off. I apologized on Robert's behalf, but she would have none of it, saying it should never have been allowed to happen. He could have done himself so much harm because he was still very ill and needed constant care.

When I went to see Robert the next day, he had had his first session with the physiotherapist, a West Indian sergeant, in the gymnasium. I quizzed him about it, subconsciously hoping to hear that he had walked or had got back the use of his arm. Of course there had been no such miracle, but he seemed more content, as though the session had got rid of some of his natural aggression. He was tired and conversation was difficult so I suggested that I go to see some of the other Scots Guards patients.

There was a company sergeant major from Left Flank in the same ward but in another side-room down the corridor. His hand had been badly smashed by a bullet. He explained that it had gone through his knuckle into his own rifle which in effect had acted as a shield. Had he not been holding it across his body he would have been shot through the chest and probably the heart.

We talked superficially after exhausting the subject of his wound. He was a laconic man, not too good with strangers, especially strange officers from the even stranger RAF. The one obvious thing we had in common was Robert and I asked clumsily what he thought of him. Robert was from Right Flank and so they had not been together in the battle for Tumbledown, but he did say that he had heard how brave Robert had been, and that it was a pity he had gone a bit too far at the end, when, after taking the machine-gun post, he had then gone on after snipers with two of his non-commissioned officers. I suggested that non-commissioned officers ran the Army anyway and in effect told the officers what to do. He would not accept that, although he said it was true that some young officers were either stupid or impetuous or both and did require a lot of guidance. Robert was not stupid, he said, but he was certainly impetuous and capable of getting himself into trouble, as he had done not only in the battle for Tumbledown but also in the hospital. Running away the day before had been very irresponsible, in his opinion, and had caused the hospital staff a lot of unnecessary anguish and trouble. I decided I did not have a great rapport with this man and left him. When I got back to Robert's room I saw that Chris had arrived so I went on up the stairs to the ward on the floor above, where Robert had told me there was a Guardsman from his platoon.

I found him sitting on his bed, his arms round his knees because he could not lean back or lie down. The whole of his back was lacerated by shrapnel wounds. I introduced myself and at first he was a bit shy, but I found it easier to break through that shyness than I had to get through to the company sergeant major. We talked of his home in Dundee and of how long he had been in the regiment. Then he said, 'Great news yesterday, sir, it went round this hospital like wildfire — "Mr Lawrence has done a bunk!" That's the man I followed through Belfast and up that bloody mountain,' he went on. 'He's amazing. We couldna keep up wi' him, he went so fast from one rock tae anither. "Where's Mr Lawrence noo? Oh, there he is, come on, let's go," and off we'd go trying to catch up. D'ye remember that film *True Grit* wi' John Wayne when he went in at the end wi' a gun in baith hands? Well, it was just like that. Mr Lawrence had a gun in baith hands at the end because he'd run out of ammunition and he picked up two Argentinian FNs, absolutely amazing. As I said, that's the man I followed through the bloody awfu' streets o' Belfast and up that damned mountain.'

This was a much better testimonial and I felt immensely proud.

Over the next few weeks I saw the sergeant major twice more and the young Guardsman at least half a dozen times, but eventually the latter's wounds healed sufficiently for him to go home on leave to Dundee. Even the sergeant major became well enough to go to the rehabilitation unit at Chessington, although there had been complications with his hand and it had taken longer to heal than they had hoped. When he left, it was by no means certain he would ever be able to hold a rifle again. God give him strength and courage and hope.

I knew my dislike of the company sergeant major was not really fair and this disturbed me. He had criticized Robert's attitude, saying in effect that although people thought a lot of his bravery they would soon get tired of him if he continued to make trouble by being aggressive and difficult. Obviously Robert could not afford to alienate anyone on whom he might have to rely, and if he never got back the use of his arm and could not walk, let alone run, then he was going to have to rely on just about everyone with whom he came into contact.

It seemed very hard to me. No one had suggested he was being aggressive and difficult on Tumbledown, except perhaps the defending Argentinians. He had not changed. In fact the miraculous thing about him was that in spite of his dreadful injury he appeared to have suffered no intellectual impairment whatsoever and there had been absolutely no change in his character. He had always been the same. Some might call him aggressive, but I preferred to think of him as positively determined. Surely this was what had enabled him to achieve what he had on Tumbledown. I remembered the orderly room colour sergeant saying he could have won money on Robert's being hurt. 'He was bound to, sir, we all knew he'd be up there in the front leading the boys.' Well, he would not be up in front physically leading the charge up the mountain any more, but I saw no reason why he could not still be there metaphorically. After a lot of thought I dismissed the sergeant major's warning.

I was pleased when Robert raised the subject himself. As an officer he was used to making decisions for others and also to giving and receiving orders, but his disability for the moment affected that position. He felt undermined and unsure of himself. I told him what the company sergeant major had said and how I had thought it through in my own mind. He seemed reassured when I agreed with his view that nothing must be allowed to stand in the way of his determination to lead as normal a life as possible. If this meant brushing aside what he might see as bureaucracy or incompetence, so be it. He was still very young, but I felt that what he had experienced in the jungles of Brunei, on the streets of Belfast and, above all, in the Falklands War qualified him to judge in a manner far beyond his years. Nevertheless, he was prepared to listen and to take advice. It was sometimes difficult, but slowly he was coming to terms with the reality of his physical limitations. If he could not climb the mountain any more, then he would have to go round it. 'Or through it, perhaps,' I suggested. We both laughed and then he said, 'Whatever, but I'll get to the other side.'

Robert Lawrence

The doctors had told me officially that I would never walk again and would most likely spend the rest of my life in a wheelchair. This was unimaginable to me. Anyone who has tried using a wheelchair with only one good hand knows that you just go round and round in circles.

Doctors were also worried, early on, about the threats of epilepsy, haemorrhaging and infection. They made constant checks on me, giving me frequent injections of antibiotics. Again and again, every time a new doctor arrived on the scene or I went to a new hospital, the same kind of tests were made, with no one seeming to be prepared to look at what was already on my records.

It was extremely tiring, and all added to the black depression most evident, as I have said, during the Maudsley period. It was then that my mother used to say to me, 'Well, Robert, at least you didn't die.' And I'd think, who was the more lucky, me or the people who died? I'd remark that perhaps I'd have been better off dead. It was a terrible thing to say, but at times then I honestly meant it.

I was determined, though, not to remain in a wheelchair for ever, determined to get up on to my feet and start walking again. It came back to pride in the end, a soldier's pride which says, 'Stuff the world, I can do it. OK, so I might have got shot through the head and I'm paralysed, but I *will* get better. And I will get to the stage where I can walk and do things for myself. Then I am going to do something with my life.' You have to keep believing in yourself and be positive. A lot of that positive thinking, the kind of positive thinking that gets people better, tends to depend on the response from everyone else. You need people to say, 'Here's a young man who is trying to get himself back on the road. We will help him all we can.' But so often, when you need those sort of people, they just aren't there.

At the Queen Elizabeth Hospital I underwent some bouts of intense physiotherapy and seemed to be making progress. But it was an almighty struggle dragging myself around and learning to walk again. I hated that wheelchair so much. Again and again, I would heave myself out of it, hoisting myself up with my good arm. Then I would stand on my good leg and attempt to grab on to something while I dragged myself round the room. As my room was so small, it got extremely frustrating at times, but eventually I learned to hop on to my bad leg and began putting on weight again.

I was getting to the stage where I really wanted to go home and attempt to get on with a normal life. I was restless, and yearning for some independence again. Instead, however, I was told that I was to go to Headley Court, an RAF rehabilitation centre. Another bloody hospital. Another place I didn't know, where I'd be stuck with more people I didn't know. The whole idea filled me with dread. I resisted it like hell.

HOME AGAIN

John Lawrence

The daily visiting continued all through July and into August. Nick went every single day, usually taking Melanie with him, Chris whenever he could, and Jean or I or both of us every day also.

Every weekend now Robert was allowed to come home. He had dispensed with the wheelchair, even though progress was slow and he could walk only a few yards. I would wheel him to the car and then return the chair to the ward before driving him back through the Friday-night traffic.

We had brought a bed down to the drawing room and during the night I could not resist coming down to see that he was all right. He always seemed to be, though he was often restless and his bed in a muddle.

I asked if he dreamed at all and he said that he sometimes did. Twice he had had what he considered to be nightmares about the battle, but in the main he was not too troubled. He upset me, though, when he explained that waking up was always disappointing because straightaway he would realize that nothing on his left side was working.

'I know you think a lot about it, Daddy, but when you're at work, and at other times, it goes out of your head. That's fine and I hope it often does, but it's with me every second of the day. Sometimes I wish I could run again, just for half an hour. That would do, then I'd come back again to this. Just half an hour, that's all, just half an hour.'

Tears were not far away for either of us, but for neither of us were they tears of bitterness.

Back in the hospital Robert pestered every day to be allowed home. He was quite prepared to go back to Woolwich for physiotherapy. Certainly that would be better than going to the Rehabilitation Unit at Headley Court. It might be a beautiful place with lovely gardens and run in a very relaxed way by the RAF, but he had heard all about it and thought it sounded dreadful. Nothing I could say would persuade him otherwise.

At last the doctors gave in and said he could come home for three weeks before going to Headley Court. I could not believe it when Robert then told us the bed could go back upstairs because he was going back to his basement flat in Chelsea. Nothing would deter him, but he did allow Jean to contact the Social Services and they agreed to put in extra railings and handles on the stairs and in the bathroom. There was not a lot more they could do, although the woman who came was triumphant one day because she had arranged to get him an electric tin-opener. It matched the electric carving knife he had bought himself. Both worried me because I found them difficult enough to work with two hands, let alone only one.

Robert had bought his flat in the January before going to the Falklands. He had furnished it well and had shown considerable imagination in the way he had organized it. Now he wanted to get down to making it something really special. This meant redecoration, clever lighting and a new floor.

His left foot often dragged and he would trip, especially over the carpet and rugs. Sometimes the ankle or the knee would stiffen involuntarily and begin to shake. When this happened he invariably fell over and of course if he was carrying coffee or even just a cigarette he would drop it. His carpet was covered in coffee stains and burns.

In the London Scottish Rugby Club there was a huge prop forward called John Richardson in one of the lower teams who specialized in tiling and laying floors. He was Scots born, the son of a sergeant major in Fort George, near Inverness, and although he'd been brought up in

South London, he frequently wore a Buchanan kilt and had 'Scotland the Brave' tatooed on his arm. He was known throughout the club as Cockney John. When I approached him about Robert's floor, he said straightaway that he would let him see some samples of parquet and give him an estimate. The whole job was done in a fortnight and it looked magnificent. Now Robert could spill all the coffee he wanted and just mop it up, with no harm done.

One day I arrived at the flat and was asked if I noticed anything special in the little hall just inside the front door. In the corner was a large pot in which Robert stood his umbrella. In it was what looked like a thumb-stick, but instead of the usual Y-shaped top it had a beautifully carved thistle-head. The thumb-rest was a short branch just below the head, and the stick was carved all the way down and decorated with silver badges and ornaments. A cord was tied at the top and looped down the length of the stick. I picked it out of the pot and admired it.

'It's Cockney John's fishing-stick,' said Robert. 'He made it himself and it's obviously his pride and joy, but he has insisted I have it. Isn't it fantastic?'

I marvelled that this tough, hard-drinking front-row forward should have been moved to part with such a personal gift. From what I knew of him he must have been very impressed by Robert.

'Do you notice anything else?'

I looked back in the hall and noticed the art deco wall light in the form of a dancing girl.

'You've had your new light installed,' I said, and switched it on. 'Very nice.'

'Yes, not bad is it? It took a bit of doing one-handed but it looks OK, doesn't it?'

Once again I could hardly believe it. Two and a half hours it had taken him, perched on a stool using his mouth and his chin as extra hands.

The following week he started painting the walls. On the Sunday evening we got a call to say he had not managed to put the radiator back properly after he had swung it down to paint behind it. Was there nothing he would not attempt, I thought, and set off in the car to see what could be done. I told the emergency plumbing service that a leak had developed and that, being disabled, Robert could not cope. They came quickly, tightened the nut with a plumber's wrench and for twenty minutes' work charged forty pounds.

We still saw Robert most days. His insistence on living alone was admirable in one sense, but worrying in another. Laundry was a constant burden. He rather fancied himself as the sartorially elegant Guards officer and would sometimes change his shirt three times in a day. Because he could not fold them properly, his clothes lay in heaps on the bedroom floor and so wearing a shirt more than once was not acceptable. The situation was not helped by the incontinence which was becoming something of a problem. Apparently he did not always get the right physical warnings and was sometimes pushed to get to the bathroom. He was also in trouble if he fell. The shock of hitting the ground usually produced a spastic involuntary evacuation of his bowel and he found this humiliating, at least to begin with. After the third or fourth time he simply stripped off, called his mother and got in a bath until she arrived to clear up the mess.

The dustbin men in Chelsea quite often work late and one evening they arrived just as Jean and I were leaving. She had done her usual tidy-up and there were two black plastic bags by the door, one full of rubbish, the other filled with laundry. I have always had a thing about dustbin men. Never upset them and always put the bin out in the place they expect to find it, otherwise they leave it behind and you are left with a pile of your own rubbish. When I heard them on the basement steps I grabbed a plastic bag and took it out to them quickly. Five minutes later I was rushing down the street trying to retrieve it and the seven shirts and soiled underwear it contained. Predictably, it had been swallowed by the lorry's voracious jaws. I explained to the foreman what I had done and he said he would look when they got to the dump. I was surprised when he said he knew all about Robert and it was the least he could do. Next day the lorry diverted from its usual round and the foreman called to say he had been unable to find anything, but for someone wounded in the Falklands it had been worth a try.

Although he lived on his own, Robert had so many friends he was seldom alone in the flat and one or more often stayed the night. Some of them were very untidy and I used to resent seeing Jean clearing up after them, but I had to be careful not to upset them. I could not bear the thought of Robert without friends, because he would always need help as far as I could tell and one day we would no longer be around and he would be old. When that day came he would need all the help he could get. (Oh, please give him strength and courage and hope.) Unless, of course, medical science had by then discovered a way of implanting a transistor in his head to replace the motor area he had lost. After all, he was only twenty-two — and look what they had discovered in the last thirty years. If they made the same sort of progress in the next thirty years, they could have him mended before he was my age and that would give him plenty of life still to live. Well, twenty years with luck, possibly more.

The transitory nature of life hit me hard and I wondered why Robert had been allowed to survive such a fearful injury. Perhaps it was because of the friendship and love that he generated around him. There was little enough in the world, after all. I had been introduced to an Argentinian girl in a pub one day and had found it difficult to talk to her in case her brother had been the one who had shot Robert. Only later did I wonder if her brother had perhaps been killed with a broken bayonet.

I had learned about the broken bayonet from Robert, although ironically it was as a result of what our hosts in South Africa had told me about his activities on Tumbledown. They had read Robert's story in the *Rand Daily Mail* and the *Cape Times* in great detail — greater than had appeared in British newspapers. They related how it was reported that he had taken the enemy machine-gun nest, leading his platoon with fixed bayonets. Out of fourteen Argentinians he had personally dealt with, three had been dispatched with the bayonet. Later, at home, I asked Robert about it and he said it was true, but the last had been difficult because the Argentinian had turned and snapped the bayonet, and a broken-off bayonet does not make a very efficient weapon. I am sure my face registered a look of horror, but he just quietly explained that the enemy soldier had been drawing his pistol – and it was either the Argentinian or him.

Robert Lawrence

I had left a friend in charge of my flat when I left for the Falklands in May. It had not proved a very satisfactory arrangement. He had left the place in one hell of a mess and had absolutely destroyed the carpet: first he had burnt it, and then he'd left it so wet that mould had begun to grow. My brothers had told me about all this while I was in Woolwich, and gave the guy concerned a bit of a hard time and kicked him out. But that still left me with the problem of laying a completely new floor, and the whole placed had to be redecorated.

My parents came along from time to time to help, and regularly checked up on me. They seemed to be coping well. At least, they were not showing signs of *not* coping. When people are being strong, as they were, I suppose you don't stop to think what might really be going through their minds.

During this leave period, my internal body clock seemed to be utterly thrown. I would sleep all afternoon and then stay up until four in the morning. Friends dropped by constantly. They would, for example, knock on the door at 7.30 a.m., then drag me out of bed for a full breakfast. Incredibly kind and sweet, of course, but also a little unnerving. And there then began this odd business of not just friends, but young men in general coming to me for advice. They asked me about things that there was no reason I should know about, or have learned from the experience I'd just had: problems over girlfriends, and things like that. They all suddenly felt they had to come and talk to me, and would hang on my every word. It was extremely odd.

At such times, I could begin to feel that I was sort of super-human — if that bullet hadn't killed me, then nothing was going to kill me. I had lived through one of the most bizarre and extreme experiences that any human being could hope to survive. I was invincible, and rather special. Then my battalion returned to Chelsea Barracks from the Falklands, and everything was a little different.

I remember being rather excited about seeing them again after three months, and I turned up at the barracks in a Panama hat, mainly to cover the shaved head. The Scots Guards had obviously had an enormous party on landing at Brize Norton, because they had numerous bottles of champagne with them when they arrived back, and the Grenadiers had also done a small 'welcome home' guard of honour for them, presenting arms as they drove in on the coaches.

The Commanding Officer got off one coach and greeted me, while all the other vehicles swung off to the other side of the parade square. Then Guardsman Joe O'Reilly, who had been my orderly once, came running over to see me, and another two Guardsmen said, 'We'll go and get Sergeant Jackson.' (Jackson was my platoon sergeant.) 'He'll keep what's left of the platoon together.' And off they went.

I remember then suddenly turning round to Joe, who had stayed with me as I limped laboriously across the parade square. And he was crying.

'What's wrong, Joe?' I asked. I couldn't understand it.

And he said, 'I just can't believe it. Of all the jerks in the battalion, why did it bloody well have to happen to you?'

It was extremely touching and I didn't know what to say. I went across and met up with the rest of my boys, but after that it all seemed like a terrible anticlimax. Following this visit, the weeks at home went by very swiftly, and then, towards the end of August, it was on to Headley Court and a whole new ball game.

RAF HEADLEY COURT

Robert Lawrence

Headley Court, near Leatherhead, in Surrey, had a beautiful house in its grounds, as my father had promised. Only,
when I arrived there, having been driven by my mother,
we were shown into a ward in this sort of semi-prefab
outbuilding instead of the main house. Inside, it was quite
bleak and dreadful, full of awful standard Army hospital
beds, and in the middle stood a ghastly Formica-topped
table with a couple of plastic sauce bottles on it.

In addition, the administration seemed to know nothing
about me. They had not received my medical records from
Woolwich and were aware only that a young officer was
arriving who had been shot through the head. They didn't
know whether I could see, hear, talk or walk. I could have
been a cabbage. For that reason, they stuck me in this
bleak observation ward instead of in the main building,
together with an old man in his sixties who had just
suffered a stroke. I was left looking at this beautiful house
opposite, this supposedly splendid wood-panelled officers'
mess, feeling really pissed off.

The staff's argument was that the wood panelling in
the main house represented a fire risk, and, should a fire
occur, somebody as ill as I was would not be able to get
out in time. My father drove up from London then, to sort
things out, and had a few blazing rows. And in the end,
after about two weeks, I was moved across to the main
house.

The usual endless tests, the prodding and the sticking in
of needles followed. Test after bloody test, because they
didn't have my records. And I think I became a cause of

considerable puzzlement to a lot of the military old guard. For a start, I looked pretty bizarre. The hair on the half of my head that had been shaved had grown back standing upright, while the rest grew normally and flat; I appeared to be sporting a light Mohican style. On top of this, I refused to wear military issue tracksuits, preferring my own instead, with a jacket on the top, and a Sony Walkman covered my ears wherever I went. You can imagine the reaction.

'Who,' these old general types would say, 'is the punk rocker hippy over there?'

But then when they found out who I was, I was suddenly excused. They would come over and, to give them their due, be very nice. I, on the other hand, just couldn't stop reacting against the whole Army set-up. I didn't care about the system any more. I had lost my fear of it. There was nothing anybody could do to me then that could compare to what had already happened, and I wasn't going to be a good boy and do as I was told, as all good young soldiers and officers should do. I knew that if I'd been marched in front of a commanding officer then, and he had said something like, 'You've been a very naughty boy, Robert, shouting at your physiotherapist, so you are going to be restricted to camp for the next two weeks as punishment,' I'd have told him to sod off. And I got to wondering how on earth I'd ever accepted all the punishments and beatings in my life before.

Arguably, I must have been pretty arrogant and big-headed. But I felt I'd done my job for the system, and if only the system would do its job as well as I had done mine, with the same degree of sacrifice, I would be looked after an awful lot better.

I lost my temper quite a few times, until eventually there appeared to be great concern as to my mental stability, and a psychiatrist kept pestering for tests. I was taken to Woolwich to undergo a week of psychiatric examination; I was given all sorts of tests, such as having to cut up cartoons and make a story out of them. Having already done a lot of similar tests before, when I passed selection for 14 Intelligence Company in Northern Ireland before the Falklands War, I completed them very quickly indeed. Then the psychiatrist testing me said, 'I'm going to give you a letter of the alphabet and start a clock. After a minute, I want you to have written down as many words beginning with that letter as you can think of.'

He gave me the letter 'S'. It was really quite laughable and must, I thought, before beginning to write, be to do with sex. So off I went, 'stockings, suspenders, sheets...' I looked upon it as a joke and went completely over the top. When I handed the test back to the psychiatrist, I was waiting for him to start laughing. But not at all. Instead he took it all totally seriously, and seemed to have no sense of humour at all.

My brother Nick kept threatening to ring him up later, to tell him that I had been a stroppy little sod since the day I was born, and that there was absolutely nothing wrong with me now. I felt I had the same personality I'd always had, but as a result of recent experiences my eyes were gradually being opened to some unpleasant realities, and that couldn't help but change me in the end.

Looking back, I realized that I had always been a bit of a romantic. Maybe it's something I inherited from my father. I had ideals, but I would always try to put them within a realistic context. I was always an individual and, in the main, I benefited from it. However, when you spend a very lengthy period in hospital, all those things about your personality that used to motivate you before just grind to a halt. Somehow you've got to find the strength from somewhere to live through this thing and get started again. You have to decide what the hell you are going to do with your life from now on; how you are going to afford to eat, pay the mortgage, and generally provide for yourself in the future.

At Headley Court, I decided that the only way I was going to get better was to look ahead to the future. But to do that I needed to know what my financial situation was

going to be. Would I receive, for instance, only a minimal
Army pension and a minimal donation from the South
Atlantic Fund? Knowing one way or the other would have
a great bearing on any future plans I might make. If I were
to get only a minimal pension and donation from the South
Atlantic Fund, it would mean that I would have to get a
job to pay the mortgage I was already committed to; one
of those desperate, nine-to-five, regularly paid safe bets.
If, on the other hand, the pension and donation turned
out to be more considerable, I would be freer to do what
I wanted to do.

Once the war in the Falklands was over, the South
Atlantic Fund administrators should have been able to sort
out cases for compensation swiftly. They knew how many
had been killed and injured, and many disabled men and
bereaved families needed to know as soon as possible the
sort of financial aid they might get in order to plan their
futures. Instead, the Fund sat on their money — which
eventually amounted to something in the order of sixteen
million pounds — for about a year and a half, telling us
nothing.

Getting an Army disability pension is also a laborious
process. Of course, I knew there was no way I could have
half my head blown away and then expect total recovery,
any more than if I had chopped off my leg, put it in a
dustbin, and seen it taken away. I would not then sit there
believing my leg was going to grow again. But the Army,
understandably I suppose, preferred to wait until I had
undergone all the medical treatment and recovery time
that would allow maximum improvement before they
were prepared to assess my pension and release me.

Meanwhile, all I could do was lie for an age in hospital,
knowing I would never be a soldier again, and wondering
what the hell else I was going to do, with the added
frustration of being kept in the dark about my financial
future.

* * *

During my time at Headley Court, I heard that there was going to be a Lord Mayor's Victory Parade for Falklands veterans, to be held in the City of London. But the wounded were not going to be allowed to take part in it. We weren't allowed to be there. I remember I was very kindly invited by Mappin and Webb to come and have lunch with them and watch from their offices, which overlooked the parade route, instead. But I just felt too disgusted.

The newspapers later reported that all the Falklands injured who were at Headley Court — about four of us, at the most — had watched the whole thing on television: 'Wounded servicemen,' one cutting I kept says, 'watched the Falklands Victory Parade proudly on Tuesday on television sets in Headley Court, the RAF rehabilitation centre. Therapy work on the patients ended early to ensure no one missed a second of the parade through the City of London. The men also had a taste of the day's events when helicopters on their way to London flew overhead. . .'

It was all absolute rubbish. An utter fabrication. I didn't stop therapy early, I certainly didn't see any helicopters fly by, and why the hell, if I hadn't been invited, should I have been watching the bloody thing proudly on television?

A month or so later, a thanksgiving ceremony for those killed or injured in the Falklands was held at St Paul's Cathedral. But although I was invited this time, I was told that I would not be allowed to wear uniform. This greatly upset me, because I saw no reason why I should not. I was an injured soldier, wounded in the course of a war, and at that time still officially in the Army. And I saw nothing to be ashamed or embarrassed about in turning up as such.

I arrived at the cathedral an hour early, in order to allow plenty of time to be helped in. I was stuck down one of the side arms of the church's cross-like interior, where I could see absolutely nothing, not even the Queen or the Royal Family when they arrived. After the service, I then had to wait well over an hour, until the procession had cleared the cathedral, before I was allowed to be removed in my wheelchair. Insult, again, to bloody injury.

I knew one could argue that the victims of war had never been well looked after. But the difference between the last two world wars, it seemed to me, and the Falklands conflict was that the former had been fought fairly close to home, had gone on for a number of years and affected the whole of the nation. Most people had either lost someone close or knew somebody who had, and everyone was involved. There just wasn't the same degree of national understanding for those who had been wounded in a brief war thousands of miles away. People either wouldn't, or couldn't, see the Falklands victims of the eighties in the same light. As a result, we were battling on our own.

* * *

One day at Headley Court I had a particularly strange visit from a major claiming to be from 5 Infantry Brigade. He wore combat kit, and a maroon beret with a Medical Corps badge on it, and asked me to come into an empty office for a chat.

'We're doing research,' he said, 'into the casevac procedure — the system of evacuating casualties from the battlefield. We want to get it right, and learn any lessons from the past that we can, for when it happens again.'

This threw me, the fact that he was already talking about the next conflict, but I explained to him that although it might have taken two and a half hours to get me off the battlefield at Tumbledown, and I had then had to wait another four and a half hours at Fitzroy hospital, there had been good reasons for it — the helicopter had been hampered by artillery fire, the hospital had justifiable priorities, and so on.

'The casevac procedure was very good, considering,' I told him. 'But what I can't understand is why I'm not getting any help now.'

The major then launched into all sorts of bizarre questions: Had I killed anyone? Had I *enjoyed* killing people. . . Had I got a real thrill out of it?

I was amazed, but screwed down my emotions all the time he was there. The second he let me go, I went into the corridor and cried my eyes out. Sally, my occupational therapist, and John, my physiotherapist, were terribly kind and comforting. Neither of them knew who this visitor was; he hadn't, apparently, asked permission to come and speak to a patient. He had just walked straight into the camp, presumably with the right ID, and asked for me. It was all very strange. I didn't understand it at all. I still don't know who he was, and I never saw him again.

Another distressing incident occurred on Battle of Britain Sunday, after I'd returned to Headley Court with my father at the end of a weekend out. It must have been about eleven o'clock at night, and I said, 'If we hurry we might get a quick drink in the officers' mess bar.'

There were a lot of RAF officers in there in uniform, with girlfriends and wives, and they'd obviously been having a bit of a do that day. My father and I began chatting quite happily to various people, and then suddenly there was this almighty outburst. A branch officer, i.e. one commissioned from the ranks, laid into me, across the whole of the mess bar, and in front of everyone, for not wearing a tie. Then he went on, 'Just because you're a Guards officer who got shot, you think you can do what the hell you like, don't you? You think you can run the bloody world. Well, you should have been in a proper war, mate. Now, get out of the mess. You're improperly dressed.'

Possibly I deserved a lot of what he said, taking into account the overall picture of my behaviour there. But I certainly didn't deserve to have it said in those particular circumstances. Everyone in the room looked disgusted. Later on, a lot of them tried to comfort me, telling me not to worry, the officer was a real jerk. But the incredible aggression of this man had left me stunned. I tried to analyse it, tried to wonder what might lie behind it. The chances were, perhaps, that he'd missed out on his own opportunities. He'd probably been too young to fight in the Second World War, and here he was now, an administrative branch officer in a medical unit in Surrey, faced with some young guy coming back from war, lording it over the place and demanding attention. That much I suppose I could understand. But it didn't help the hurt go away.

DECORATED FOR LEADERSHIP AND COURAGE

John Lawrence

While Robert was still at Headley Court, the Falklands awards were published in the *London Gazette*, on 8 October 1982.

The two Victoria Crosses naturally got all the publicity, but there were only sixteen Military Crosses awarded, five Royal Marines and eleven Army, and Robert had one of them. Almost better than that, as far as he was concerned, was the fact that his platoon sergeant, Sergeant Jackson, and one of his Guardsmen, Pengelly, both won the Military Medal.

Major John Kiszely, who had commanded Left Flank, also won the Military Cross; the CO, Lieutenant-Colonel Mike Scott, was awarded the Distinguished Service Order; Guardsman Reynolds from Headquarters Company won the Distinguished Conduct Medal posthumously; and Company Sergeant Major Nicol also won the DCM.

There were fourteen from the battalion mentioned in Dispatches, and that was the lot from the Scots Guards.

'Not bad,' said Robert, 'we have never been generous in dishing out the medals. I think you really have to earn it in the Scots Guards, not like some others I could mention.'

I suggested that this was perhaps a little unfair, even arrogant, but when I read the citations in the *London Gazette* I had to admit that those written for Paras and Marines tended to be much more flamboyant than those for the Scots Guards.

'On the night of 13th/14th June, on the island of East Falklands, the 2nd Battalion Scots Guards attacked well-entrenched positions on the craggy ridge feature of

Tumbledown Mountain, seven kilometres to the west of Port Stanley. Lieutenant Lawrence and his Platoon were amongst leading elements in the assault.

'As they came up to an area of prominent rocky crags they came under intense fire from an enemy machine-gun position. Lieutenant Lawrence, to the fore throughout, immediately led an attack. Throwing grenades on to the enemy position as he went, he continued in the heat of the fire fight to exhort his Platoon to follow him in the assault. His attacking group destroyed the enemy.

'Firm on that position, he gathered up a handful of his men and began to work his way along the ridge to engage an enemy sniper. As they closed and just before he could attack, Lieutenant Lawrence was severely wounded.

'His actions were an outstanding example of leadership under fire and courage in the face of the enemy.'

Over and over I read it, again and again. There had been four snipers, not one, and Robert with his two NCOs had got three of them before the fourth shot him. There was no mention of bayonet fighting in Robert's citation, but there was in John Kiszely's. Robert's seemed so terribly bland and yet it had been sufficient to get through the awards committee. He said he was not surprised by the lack of detail in the citation because no one apart from his platoon had been there to see exactly what he did. Left Flank had been held up, which was why he had been called up to lead his platoon, followed by Mark Mathewson's, in a right-flanking attack. It was only just getting light as he was shot, so how anyone knew what was going on he had no idea.

Some time afterwards, Jeremy Campbell-Lamerton, a member of the London Scottish 1st XV, who had commanded the mortar platoon at the rear of the battalion, told me that from where he had been he could follow Robert's classic platoon attack through night glasses from the pattern of the fire. Also, General Sir Digby Raeburn, who was late Scots Guards and had finished his career as Governor of the Tower of London, told me that Robert's citation was as good as any won by a Scots Guardsman in either the First or the Second World War. That seemed very generous to me, but I was not going to argue.

There was great excitement in the family and congratulations to Robert came flowing in. A glowing letter from the United States Defense Attaché in London was particularly well worded, but I found it ironic in the light of the performance of Jean Fitzpatrick, the US Ambassador to the United Nations. To my mind she had totally failed to support the UK, being concerned only with US relations with South and Central America. Much later I was to learn that the Americans had in fact given a lot of quiet, almost undercover support to us.

In early November, after numerous enquiries, we received details of Robert's investiture by Her Majesty the Queen. It was to be in December and he could take both his parents as guests. Some weeks before then, however, there was to be another ceremony at Buckingham Palace, at which the three Household Division regiments that had served in the Falklands were to parade for Her Majesty. The three Colonels would present South Atlantic medals with Falklands rosettes to their respective regiments: the Duke of Edinburgh to the Blues and Royals; the Prince of Wales to the Welsh Guards; and the Duke of Kent to the Scots Guards.

We picked Robert up in good time and he insisted that he would be able to walk to the palace from the Wellington Barracks parade ground where we had to park. It was a bitterly cold day and in spite of his greatcoat Robert was frozen. He struggled manfully, but the walk was too far for him. He rested every twenty yards and I stretched his left arm which was curling up badly with both the cold and the over-exertion.

When we got to the palace we were shown round to the lawns at the rear and were ushered to three rows of folding wooden chairs. The front row was for the wounded and the back two rows for the guests. Robert was placed first in the row at the far end and we were

ight behind him. Alongside him were the rest of the Scots
Guards wounded who were still not fit enough to parade.
There had been forty-three wounded originally, including
a major and another subaltern, both of whom were now
fully mobile and on parade. There was a Welsh Guards
subaltern who had received bad burns during the attack
on the *Sir Galahad*, but otherwise, as far as we could see,
Robert was the only other wounded officer.

A Welsh Guardsman came past with his pretty girlfriend
and others. There seemed to be a great fuss as they were
shown to seats further up the row. Robert looked round at
us and said, 'Aren't you glad I'm not like that poor devil?'

We most certainly were. The Welshman was Guardsman Simon Weston and he had survived the most incredible burns when the *Sir Galahad* had been hit at Bluff
Cove. The Scots Guards had gone round the island from
San Carlos in a landing craft. It had been a ghastly journey,
but they had survived it and had already landed when the
Sir Galahad carrying the Welsh was hit. Robert told
us that the smell of burning flesh was quite the worst
memory he had of the whole war.

Jean and I shuddered and gave thanks that bad as Robert
was, he was not disfigured like Simon Weston. God, give
him strength and courage and hope.

A few months afterwards I met Simon at Cardiff Arms
Park where he was a guest of the Welsh Rugby Union at
the Wales v. Scotland match. We had a beer together
after the match and talked a little about the Falklands. He
had been the Welsh Guardsman whose parents had been
waiting so long at Brize Norton. He knew all about Robert
though they had never met.

'Some officer, your son,' he said. 'I've talked to several
of his fellows on the hospital ship and they say the great
thing about him was that he would never ask them
to do anything that he hadn't thoroughly worked out
beforehand. If it was risky then he'd explain it, but they
were always ready to give it a go because they knew he'd
give them the best chance of coming through. What I hear

of him he's a good boy and should have got more than an MC.'

I was thrilled by his words, and thanked him for being so generous in the light of his own terrible injuries and his own bravery.

By the time the parade was fully mustered we were absolutely frozen. I tried to stretch Robert's arm again for him, but it was difficult to do unobtrusively and he waved me away. The Scots Guards medical officer appeared and stationed himself at the end of the row next to Robert.

The royal party arrived on the scene, and after the royal salute they began the task of presenting a medal to each man on parade. It was going to take an age and I was worried about Robert standing in the bitter cold. Several times I thought he was going to pass out, but eventually the doctor told him to sit down. The rest of the wounded followed suit.

We stood again as the Duke of Edinburgh approached followed by the Duke of Kent, General Langley and the usual entourage. Among them were the Lieutenant Colonel Commanding and the Regimental Adjutant. As they reached us the doctor saluted and Prince Philip asked him if he had been wounded in the Falklands. He explained that he was the medical officer and it was those in the front row who were the wounded and had been in the fighting.

I read in the paper the next day that the parade was the third of six functions that the Duke of Edinburgh had attended that day. No wonder he had seemed confused by the doctor; he was still talking to him when he pinned on Robert's medal, hardly even looking at him. I felt disappointment for Robert. However, the Duke of Kent knew him by name immediately and spoke to him at length. Then, looking up at Jean and me, he said, 'He's looking much better than when we last met.' I agreed, and felt much better too.

On the morning of the investiture we were allowed to drive through the palace gate and park in the inner courtyard. I stopped under the portico to let Jean and

Robert get out of the car. When I had parked, a policeman looked underneath, in the boot and under the bonnet before I could return to join them. On the steps we were told there would be official photographers in the courtyard afterwards, and naturally Jean was keen that we should have a photograph taken. I explained that I had arranged through their rugby correspondent that the Press Association photographer would take one of us.

Inside the palace we were ushered to the left and up the staircase along the corridor to the Throne Room where the investiture was to take place. Two Gurkha officers were standing on duty on either side of one of the side-doors. I thought of the *Arabian Nights* and of slaves posted outside the harem of the Caliph, but it was only a momentary thought. These were not slaves, they were not even Her Majesty's subjects, yet they were loyal and brave and represented some of the best troops in the British Army. Some, of course, had fought in the Falklands.

At the next door we were greeted by a pipe major. From his collar badge I thought he was a Gordon Highlander but his kilt was red Royal Stewart, not green with the yellow check of the Gordons. I stopped and asked what regiment he was in and he confirmed that it was the Gordon Highlanders. I was puzzled and then realized that of course he was wearing Royal Stewart; he was the Queen's Piper.

As we came to the Throne Room a familiar face appeared. Group Captain John Slessor had been my commanding officer at Odiham when I was first promoted to the rank of wing commander. He had commanded the station while I administered it. He took a serious interest in the flying, but he also thought it was fun. We had got on very well and had worked closely in adjoining offices in the station headquarters.

John's face beamed as he saw us. 'Hello, I'm so glad you're in good time. It's frightfully difficult to keep seats for people, but Roy has been hanging on to a couple in the second row for as long as he can.'

We thanked him and walked to the front of the room where Air Marshal Sir Roy Austen-Smith was standing smiling at the end of the second row of red-velvet-seated gold chairs. Roy had been a flying instructor at Cranwell when I was a cadet and had married the sister of someone in the entry below me. She was great fun. She had once climbed back into the college through my ground-floor bedroom window at the end of the graduation ball. They now lived near us and she recounted the story with great hilarity whenever we were in the same company, I always being careful to explain that she had only been looking for a bacon sandwich.

Roy and John were extra equerries to the Queen and it was comforting to see their familiar uniforms and faces.

The band of the Welsh Guards were playing while we waited for the investiture to begin. We had been among the first to arrive, but the room very quickly filled and through the gap to the left we saw the first of those lining up to receive their decorations and awards. The queue stretched down the outside ante-room, appearing again at the back of the Throne Room behind us and then disappearing out of the far door where we had come in. Robert had left us soon after entering the palace and was as yet not to be seen.

John Slessor had very kindly given us his working programme which had all the names in the order in which they would be presented to the Queen. Among them was Terry Waite, special envoy for the Archbishop of Canterbury. There was also Alun Williams, the Welsh rugby commentator. Robert was about ninetieth in the list and I wondered how he would cope with standing for all that time.

The two Gurkha officers appeared, marching slowly through the archway to our right. Behind them we saw Her Majesty saying goodbye to a family of people who, like all of us, were clearly dressed in their Sunday best. John had explained that the Queen always saw privately

beforehand the families of those who had been decorated posthumously. I believe these were the relatives of
Guardsman Reynolds and again I gave thanks for Robert's
survival. The Gurkhas had halted at the entrance to the
Throne Room, but now set off again, moving in unison
like toy soldiers, their heads and eyes absolutely still,
looking straight ahead. They were not slow-marching in
the traditional manner with arms to the sides and toes
pointed down. Instead they were marching slowly, their
arms swinging to exactly the same small angle in front and
behind.

Everyone in the room stood up as the Queen entered
followed by the Lord Chamberlain and two equerries.
They mounted the first step of the dais and the Queen
turned to face us. The band played the National Anthem
and the Gurkhas saluted, they being the only ones present
wearing hats.

Behind the Queen, to her left, was a table with all the
medals and ribbons set out in order. One of the equerries
stood beside it ready to hand the appropriate medal to
Her Majesty. On her right, behind a microphone, was Lord
Maclean, late Scots Guards, the Lord Chamberlain of the
Household. He was to read out the names.

The new knights came first and for them a small velvet
stool was placed against the first step on the dais in front
of the Queen. They were summoned one by one by the
Lord Chamberlain to walk out in front of the audience
and stop in front of the stool. There they turned to face
Her Majesty, bowed from the neck only and, taking one
step forward, knelt with one knee on the stool with the
head still bowed. The equerry handed the Queen a naked
sword with which she lightly touched the recipient on each
shoulder. Then, exchanging the sword for the circlet or ribbon of the Order, she placed that round the new knight's
neck. He rose, bowed again from the neck and shook hands
with the Queen. To each one she said something by way of
congratulations or encouragement. Among the words she
was to say to Robert when his turn came were, 'We are so

pleased you are fit enough to have been able to come.'

I wondered how fit he was feeling now, having been standing for so long. Half an hour had gone by but the table still seemed to be full of ribbons and crosses. There were ladies who had worked for charity, men who were successful industrialists, diplomats, civil servants and every now and then officers, non-commissioned officers and servicemen. Terry Waite appeared in the archway, towering to his six foot seven inches, a kindly face above the huge black beard. Even with the benefit of the stepped dais Her Majesty still had to reach up, almost on tiptoe, to hang the medal on the little hook that, like all those being invested, he had had sewn on to his jacket beforehand.

Among the knights at the beginning had been Rear Admiral John Woodward and Major General Jeremy Moore. 'Sandy' Woodward had been the Force Commander of the whole Falklands campaign and Jeremy Moore had been the Land Forces Commander.

The rank of commander is usually the next below that of knight in an order of chivalry, the one above that being Knight Commander and above that Knight Grand Cross. All very confusing, but at last we seemed to be through the Commanders of the Bath and the Commanders of St Michael and St George. I had a little chuckle as I recalled CMG, call me God; KCMG kindly called me God; GCMG, God calls me God.

The deep crimson of the Bath ribbons gave way to the brighter, lighter red of the Most Excellent Order of the British Empire. Three times in his career my father had been put up for the Order, once to be a Member, twice to be an Officer. The first time was in 1938 when he commanded the first ever operational radar station in the world. It was at Swingate on the cliffs of Dover along from the castle. There were three other stations at that time, Ventnor on the Isle of Wight, Dunkirk near Canterbury and Canewdon near Southend, but Swingate was operational first by a matter of days. My father reckoned there was one MBE between the four and they drew

ots. Canewdon won. He thought that might have been
worth winning, but not the OBE for which he was twice
recommended. 'Other Bs' Efforts' he always called it.

At last, after an hour and a half, Robert appeared at
the head of the queue. He was dressed in blue patrols
with the red stripe down the side of the trousers and
the small buttons in their sets of three glinting in the
lights. Around his waist was a crimson sash and on his
chest three ribbons were already in place. The South
Atlantic Star, its blue, white and green all running into
each other like the ocean, had the small silver rosette in
its centre to denote that the wearer had actually landed
on the Falklands. Next came the General Service medal
with Northern Ireland clasp, green, purple, green in
even-width stripes. Lastly, nearest the centre of his tunic,
also in even-width stripes, the white, purple, white of the
Military Cross.

He looked pale and tired and I noticed that his left
hand was beginning to claw and his arm to curl up. He
was trying to stretch it and I desperately wanted to go
and help him. Six Distinguished Service Crosses came one
after another. The Captain of HMS *Ardent* had won one
of them, and I knew Robert had been on board his ship
for a party because the battalion had adopted *Ardent*
sometime before the campaign. The ship had been sunk
by Argentinian aircraft. Unusually, another commander,
Royal Navy, had won the Air Force Cross as well as
the DSC. Equally unusual was the fact that a Royal Air
Force flight lieutenant had won the DSC, which is still
predominantly a naval decoration.

'To be decorated with the Military Cross.'

This was it, just two to go.

'Captain William Andrew McCracken, the Royal Regiment of Artillery.'

I remembered the name. He had been in a forward
observation post in the battles for Mount Longdon and
Wireless Ridge. One to go.

'Captain Aldwin James Glendinning Wight, Welsh Guards.'

He too had been forward, but frighteningly so — behind enemy lines for twenty-six days.

At last.

'Lieutenant Robert Alasdair Davidson Lawrence, Scots Guards.'

He straightened his left arm with one final pull and stepped out from the archway. There were fourteen paces to go before he would halt and turn to face the Queen. Each one looked as though it were agony. For an hour and a half he had been waiting, moving forward in the queue just a few inches at a time, getting more and more stiff. Now in front of this large audience and, above all, in front of his sovereign he had to move his broken body in some semblance of soldierly fashion. I prayed that his ankle would not turn or his knee go into spasm and throw him sprawling on to the red carpet. After all this time waiting patiently in the queue, he probably wanted to find a lavatory, and if he fell it would be dreadfully embarrassing.

Robert did not fall. The effort was written all over his pale face, but his head was high and he did not falter. The Queen placed the medal on the little brass hook that the regimental tailor had sewn just above the three ribbons. She shook his right hand and spoke to him, her lovely smile warm, full of sympathy and, I believe, full of pride for one of her own young officers.

Instinctively Robert moved to step back and this time I thought he was going to fall. Stepping backwards was not in his repertoire, but he remembered in time and, after bowing from the neck, did a sort of shuffle turn on the spot and limped away through the far archway.

The next in the queue was already in front of the Queen as Robert disappeared from view, but there were only fifteen more after Robert and then we all stood as the Queen left, led by the two Gurkhas, to return to her private apartments.

As we ourselves left, I looked once more at the room in which we had sat for the past two hours. It was almost too magnificent to take in, but I have a lasting memory of gold and red and crystal all glowing and sparkling in a vast space of light.

I came down to earth, as it were, realizing I too could do with using a lavatory. The chances of finding such a mundane facility in a real palace seemed remote, but there had been a cloakroom where Robert had left his uniform cap and I was pleased to learn that there was a lavatory behind it. As I went in I bumped into General Sir Jeremy Moore. He was looking back over his shoulder saying goodbye to someone as he was coming out of the door. It was Robert.

We picked up his cap at the desk and he put it between his knees to give a quick buff to the peak. He made sure the cap star was straight and in the middle of the red and white checked hat band, and then carefully placed it on his head.

As we went down the steps outside the front door, the Lord Chamberlain stepped forward to block our way.

'I always enjoy investitures,' he said, 'but never more than when someone from my own regiment is decorated. We are very proud of you, Robert, and I thought you did awfully well today.'

Robert acknowledged the compliment and I too murmured my appreciation, but when he had gone, Robert told us that the Lord Chamberlain had once got one of his friends into trouble when he had been on Queen's Guard. No compliment was going to make up for that.

To our left an enormous queue had formed waiting for the official photographer. Robert explained that there was no way he could possibly queue any more that day. Jean looked utterly crestfallen.

There were several press photographers around but their interest seemed to be solely in the Admiral and the General and in a group of four naval officers, one of whom was the Captain of HMS *Ardent*. It seemed that they had all commanded ships in the Falklands.

I was cross that no one appeared to be interested in the only one of the heroes present who had actually been wounded. I asked one photographer if he was from the Press Association but he said he was from the *Evening Standard*.

'Oh,' I said, 'you must know Barry Newcombe the rugby correspondent.'

Fortunately, he did, and when I explained our predicament he agreed to take just one photograph. He promised to give it to Barry. I had to telephone some days later, but it now stands proudly on the bookcase in the drawing room. The medal itself does not show up very well because the flash rebounded from it, but the purple stripe in the ribbon can just be seen in the middle of the open case that Robert is holding in time-honoured pose. Jean looks very smart and lovely, with her Scots Guards brooch showing up well against her black velvet coat, but Robert appears pale and tired and his left arm and fingers have curled. It was quite an ordeal for him that day, almost worth another medal.

GETTING MOBILE

John Lawrence

After a month at Headley Court Robert told us they were
thinking of discharging him at the end of October when
he had completed eight weeks. I could not understand
it and was very disappointed, so I telephoned the senior
neurologist. A Cornishman of wing commander rank, he
sounded very pleasant and was clearly a very knowledge-
able specialist. To my great dismay his prognosis was not
good. Robert would always limp, would never be able to
walk more than eighty to a hundred metres at a time and
his left arm would never work. The only slight possibility
was that he would learn a few 'trick' movements. I knew
that by exerting himself almost to the limit he could make
his arm move about two inches. It also came up in a spastic
movement if he yawned, so presumably if he was prepared
to behave like a circus animal he could lift it on demand
simply by yawning.

Nevertheless, we were assured that Robert would gradually learn to manage with just two fully serviceable limbs.
Almost certainly there would be no actual improvement in
the damaged two, but he would learn to adapt sufficiently
to be able to cope with life. Hopefully his left arm would
not curl up or the fingers of his hand claw. So far that
had not happened, at least not as a permanent feature.
He spent hours stretching his arm, hand and fingers.
Whenever he could he would get other people to do it for
him, but otherwise he tried to do as much for himself as
he could.

When, at the end of the eight weeks, Robert left
Headley Court and moved back into his basement flat,

he returned to duty at Chelsea Barracks for three or four days a week. He was given various jobs and on one occasion took a platoon on the ranges at Pirbright for their annual marksman qualification. Apparently he took the test himself, one-handed. The senior non-commissioned officers, bursting with admiration but afraid for his own and everyone else's safety, resolved to make sure he was not given another opportunity for live-round range work.

Robert was allotted a young Guardsman orderly to look after him at his flat. His name was Hamilton and he was married, living in married quarters at Chelsea. He was marvellous and was able to come to the flat most days. His first priority was Robert's uniforms, suits and shoes. As a Guards officer Robert's turn-out had to be immaculate and Hamilton took a personal pride in ensuring that it always was.

At first, Robert spent much of his free time in his flat, but he now had a new girlfriend, Tanya, and as his friendship with her deepened he began to spend more time away from it.

Tanya was stunning. She was petite with long, long hair which she could sit on, huge dark eyes — the Eastern promise sort — a pretty figure and a delightful personality. Robert had met her at Headley Court, but had not taken her out while there. Her father was a squadron leader in the Royal Air Force and very soon in my initial conversation with her I identified him as someone I had met in Hong Kong some sixteen years before. She was delighted and so was Robert to establish immediately even so tenuous a connection.

Tanya was training to be an actress at the Guildford School of Drama, but had begun her career as a ballet dancer. Unfortunately, she had wrecked her knee very badly and an operation to replace the ligaments had not been successful. Through her father she had gone to Headley Court to try and get it right.

She had a particularly caring nature and seemed very fond of Robert. Although she chose to wear old second-hand Victorian clothes and so to my eyes often looked a bit of a mess, she was in fact very good at keeping his flat tidy and generally fussing over him. He obviously loved it and made the most of it, but she had a flat of her own in Guildford, which she shared with two other girls from the School of Drama, and so could be in Chelsea only at the weekends. It was not long before Robert was in Guildford for much of the week. His own interest in the theatre was developing and he would often spend the night on the sofa after watching Tanya and her flatmates' plays or helping backstage after joining in one of their parties.

One evening he decided not to stay and persuaded Tanya to return to Chelsea with him on the train. They set off for the station at about twenty to eleven to catch the last train up to London. One of the other girls decided to go with them. Just short of the station Tanya remembered something she had left behind and ran back to the flat, leaving Robert and the other girl waiting in the street.

A group of youths appeared, noisy and reeling drunkenly. Robert turned his back and went on talking to the girl. He was wearing his dark-blue overcoat and on his head a large navy-blue fedora. It was definitely theatrical and a shade flamboyant, but it had a practical purpose as well. Although his scar had healed, his hair was still growing and he really did look extraordinary, with long hair that lay down on the left side of his head and short hair that stood straight up on the right. Underneath it all there was still a six-by-two-inch hole in the side of his skull and for a joke he would sometimes invite people to watch the scalp that covered it pulsating in time with his heartbeat.

One of the drunks could not resist the hat and snatched it from Robert's head as he went past. He ran off up the street, jeering and caterwauling. Robert turned and in his best parade-ground voice demanded the return of his property. Almost instinctively the youth stopped in his tracks, suggesting by so doing that he might have been a soldier, perhaps a recruit from the Guards Depot at Pirbright or a Para from Brookwood.

'So you want your lovely hat, do you?' He staggered back towards Robert and when about three yards short of him threw the hat on the ground at his feet. Robert bent to pick it up and was felled with a left hook which connected just in front of his right ear. He fell on to his paralysed left side, unable to break his fall. He rolled back to his right to get some purchase from the good side of his body and the boot came in, just above the right ear. Another inch and a half and it would have smashed through the hole in his skull.

The drunks ran off to the station as Tanya arrived, out of breath, having seen what had happened. The two girls helped Robert to his feet and they set off for the station as fast as they could. A train was pulling out as they got there and there was no sign of the drunks. They explained to the ticket collector what had happened. He fetched a British Rail policeman and they went through the story again.

The next day in an attempt to expose the culprit the police gave the story to the press. The newspapers loved it and the headlines were graphic to say the least. The local *Surrey Comet* was perhaps the most factual and least sensational: 'Brutal attack on disabled hero of Falklands War'. The so-called quality papers tucked it away inside with 'Disabled soldier is beaten up', but the tabloids gave the story considerable prominence. Above a photograph of Robert, *The Sun* proclaimed 'Thug attacks disabled Falklands War hero' in huge black headlines and then a secondary headline below said 'News upsets Queen'. The *Daily Mirror* excruciatingly proclaimed 'Lawrence of Argentina takes a tumble'.

These were not the first stories about Robert to appear in the papers. Lady Olga Maitland had written about him in the *Sunday Express* when he had first been wounded. We had been embarrassed because somehow or other she had heard the story of the Queen expressing her concern to me about Robert at the Test Match. The press have a job to do, of course, but their invasion of privacy can sometimes be disturbing.

Christopher, Nicholas and Robert Lawrence as children.

left Robert aged 10 (see page 4).
above Robert outside Lord's, shortly bef
his final head operation, July 1983.

top The platoon commanders and platoon sergeants of Right Flank,
2nd Battalion Scots Guards, on their way to the Falklands on the
QE2 (Robert crouching, far left).
bottom Scots Guards dig trenches under shell fire.

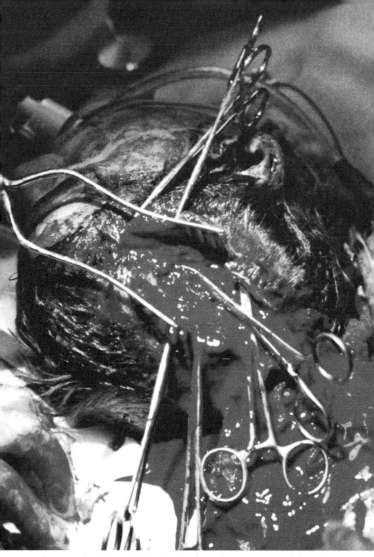

above and right top Robert's head on the operating table at Fitzroy, seven hours after he was shot (see page 152).
right bottom The wound is sealed.

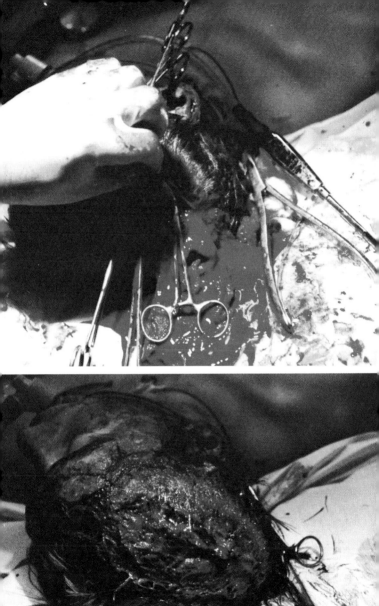

top Tumbledown Mountain.
bottom Evacuation of casualties on the morning of 14 June 1982:
'walking wounded' make their way towards a Scout.

top Robert (left) and actor Colin Firth during rehearsals for the
BBC film *Tumbledown*.
bottom Robert (second from right) took an active part in the
making of *Tumbledown*.

top John, Jean and Robert Lawrence outside Buckingham Palace, following Robert's investiture, December 1982 (see page 112).

left Robert an●
below Baby C

Three months after the attack in Guildford, Robert was again in the papers. He had been greatly shaken by the incident and argued strongly that if he could be allowed to drive, the chances of such a thing recurring would be greatly reduced.

Robert Lawrence

The arguments for my being allowed to drive seemed logical, but getting anyone to agree to it proved to be another stumbling block. After initially asking around Headley Court, I was told that the risk of epilepsy was too great. I assured them that I had never, ever, either before or after my injury, suffered an epileptic fit and that almost a year had now passed since I had been shot. Help, however, was not forthcoming and eventually it was my mother, a senior college lecturer, in other words a civilian in full-time employment, who found out about a mobility centre in Banstead which undertook special driving tests. Except when actually having children, my mother has always worked. She has been an absolutely wonderful mother but I think she is the sort of woman who is a better person for working rather than staying at home all day. And, of course, by working she has helped towards ensuring that we have all had the best possible education and a lovely home.

She had to take a day off work to get me to Banstead. Then it was up to me to pay the fifty-pound fee out of my own pocket. I didn't think it would have been asking too much for any of the services' establishments to have organized both.

After I had undergone various medical tests, psychiatric tests and reaction tests, as well as the actual driving evaluation, for which I drove round a circuit in an adapted car, the Banstead centre gave me the go-ahead. My original driving licence had been lost in the Falklands, so I sent off an application for a replacement in January 1983. Being a good honest citizen, I informed the staff at Swansea DVLC about my disability, and told them that I could obviously drive only an automatic car with power-assisted steering and so on. I then sat back and waited.

At this time I was beginning to look to a future outside the Army, possibly in the theatre. When I moved back into my flat from Headley Court, I had been given the position of second-in-command of my own company in the Scots Guards, and would go into Chelsea Barracks a few days a week to see what I could do. But it soon occurred to me that I wasn't cut out for it, realistically. I couldn't take part in any of the exercises or any of the normal work routine and, although some people welcomed my presence, and seemed very happy to see me coming in, I knew it would never work out.

I was spending more and more time travelling to Guildford to be with Tanya and her friends, so when I was informed, via the Scots Guards at Chelsea, that British Leyland were kindly offering a free Metro car to every soldier injured in the Falklands conflict, I was delighted. I did, however, explain to British Leyland that while I didn't wish to sound ungrateful, or to appear to be looking a gift-horse in the mouth, I didn't want a Metro; it didn't suit my injury. No problem, they replied; you can choose a car from the Leyland range that does.

As instructed, I turned up at Henley's garage in Barnes at the allotted time. They were a nice bunch of people at the garage, and tested me out first on the Triumph Acclaim, the next one up in the range. I opened the driver's door, sat down on the seat and swung my legs in, but just as I went to lean back a little, I banged my head hard on the car roof, which gave me a bit of a fright. So the Triumph Acclaim was taken away and an Austin Princess brought over. Unfortunately, in that, my left leg jammed underneath the steering wheel and I couldn't move. Then I was shown a Rover 2000, a much bigger car, with a 2-litre engine.

In the end, I opted to pay the difference between the 2-litre Rover and a 2.3-litre model with electric windows and a sun-roof. The salesmen seemed quite happy with this, and so was I.

Instructions came from Chelsea Barracks that I was to wear uniform — 'service dress with medals', to be precise — to receive the keys of the car. It was ironic that uniform had not been considered suitable for a victory parade but was thought to be perfectly appropriate for publicity stunts over free cars.

About four or five other injured Scots Guards came with me to receive the vehicles on offer, but I was the only officer among them. It was all done to launch the new Maestro range in the classic showbiz way. There was a huge paper wall in the garage showroom through which the new Maestro was to be driven — although unfortunately the one they had picked to do this stalled. Then the actor Derek Nimmo was to present us with our keys for publicity purposes — not the *real* keys to our cars, mind, as these wouldn't be available for another few weeks. It was all a bit false, but we didn't mind at all. We were happy to play our part, because they had been kind enough to give us free cars. Or so we thought.

My new Rover, courtesy of Leyland, was eventually delivered to Chelsea Barracks, for which I was very grateful. Until, that is, about a year later, when my donation from the South Atlantic Fund finally arrived. From it had been deducted £11,500 for the car, minus the standard eighteen per cent discount for disabled drivers. The free car was no free car after all. With regret I realized that nothing had been put in writing about this so-called 'gift' arrangement and that I, together with all the other Falklands victims in the publicity stunt, had just been used. The incident highlighted, I think, the exploitation for publicity purposes that many Falklands casualties faced.

John Lawrence

Delivery of the Rover took a couple of months, during which Robert was to return to Headley Court for further physiotherapy and rehabilitation, in the faint hope that some further improvement could be achieved. Henley's very kindly lent him an automatic Cortina for this period. It was quite old and not very smart, but it was 'wheels' and he was mobile again.

There was another Falklands casualty inmate at Headley Court when Robert arrived back, a young pilot who had ejected when his Harrier had been shot down and had hurt his back. He had also been the only British prisoner-of-war, and life had not been easy for him. Unfortunately, although Headley was very good at dealing with physical strains such as this pilot's, it was not so good at sorting out mental stress. Robert explained this quite forcibly and with the minimum of sympathy. He also decided fairly soon into his second sojourn at Headley that no one there could do very much more for him.

The uncertainty of his future in the Army was definitely playing on his mind. The possibility of his transferring to the Royal Army Ordnance Corps had been suggested, but that was of no interest to him. A job in the royal household could probably he found, but kind as this offer might be, and although such a job would certainly be an honour, it would not provide the excitement and challenge that a twenty-two-year-old holder of the Military Cross needed to keep him going. Why could he not still enter the Intelligence Company and work under cover? After all, what better disguise than to have a genuinely useless left arm and a spastic left leg?

No one at Headley Court could help with this problem and so we contacted the Scots Guards. The battalion had been allowed very little relaxation after their return from the South Atlantic. Their principal role was with NATO and they were soon working up again to meet that commitment. The problem was therefore left largely to Regimental Headquarters to sort out.

There is no doubt that the regiment genuinely looks upon itself as a family and in most respects this gives it an extraordinary strength. It also draws strength from being part of the élite Household Division, but this inevitably causes envy in other parts of the Army. In the past, the Guards regiments were something of a law unto themselves, but unfortunately those days have largely gone and they are in danger of being swallowed up by the great Army machine. Consequently, the enforcement of regulations by faceless people in the vast bureaucracy of the Ministry of Defence can often be unsympathetic. Moreover, extracting proper information from the machine can be extremely difficult. This was certainly the case for Regimental Headquarters Scots Guards in their efforts to sort out Robert's future.

His financial future was still equally uncertain. Straight after the Argentinian surrender a South Atlantic Fund had been set up to deal with all the thousands of pounds being sent in by the general public as donations to help the wounded and bereaved. The response had been spontaneous, and well before Christmas the Fund had reached over ten million pounds. Various articles had appeared in newspapers about the Fund money and how it would be spent, but Robert had heard nothing until receiving an interim payment of ten thousand pounds out of the blue through the Guards Charitable Fund. There was no explanation other than that it had to be paid this way. No one would say if there would be more to come or, if so, roughly how much. It was all very haphazard, although of course Robert was delighted with the gift and we were all greatly appreciative of the generosity of the general public.

The administration of appeal funds is difficult and their distribution even more difficult. The problems encountered with the Penlee Lifeboat Fund were a good illustration of this. It seems ironic that in the first place such funds stem from kindness, generosity, admiration and love and yet so often in the end generate a great deal of envy, greed, criticism and anger.

Although on being selected for intelligence before the Falklands War Robert had agreed to become a regular

officer serving to pensionable age, his visit to the South
Atlantic had interrupted the paperwork and of course
when he was wounded it was all shelved. In consequence
he was still a short service officer with a discharge date set
for 3 August 1983.

As a short-service officer he would not normally qualify
for a pension, but now there was clearly an obligation to
pay him a disability pension. In December I had asked
about it, but although I was given general assurances that
he would of course get a pension, no one could actually
confirm it or say how much it would be. This uncertainty
was a great worry and the size of the South Atlantic Fund
and how much Robert might receive from it therefore
assumed greater significance for us.

In spite of all the uncertainty, Robert was nevertheless
cheerful, and looked forward to the delivery of his new
car. Then, in the second week of March, the whole picture
was shattered by the arrival of a letter from the DVLC
in Swansea. It told him that after careful consideration of
his case it was regretted that his driving licence would be
withdrawn from 19 March 1983, which was the following
Tuesday, five days away. No reason was given nor any
hope of appeal or date of review.

Robert almost went berserk with anger, frustration and
disappointment. At Headley Court they were sympathetic, and the specialist wrote to Swansea explaining that in
his view withdrawing his licence would do Robert untold
emotional damage. He also suggested to Robert that the
regiment might be able to help. Robert took up the
suggestion and went off to London straightaway in the
Cortina. After all, he was allowed to drive it until the next
Tuesday.

The BBC had recently been in touch with Regimental
Headquarters seeking permission to interview Robert.
They were planning a number of interviews with Falklands
casualties and had heard that he was one of the few
officers to have been really severely wounded. Permission
had been granted, but after Robert's visit that day it was

withdrawn. He had unleashed a tirade that had shaken the sedate routine of Headquarters to its foundations. Being able to drive was at the heart of his recovery. If he could drive he would continue to fight his disability; if not, then he might just as well sit in a wheelchair for the rest of his life and let other people look after him. Yet no one, as far as he was concerned, was prepared to help him secure his driving licence. It was his mother who had found out about the Mobility Centre, and he who had paid the fifty-pound fee. Now some faceless doctor in Swansea, at the stroke of a pen, had stopped him driving for ever — and the Rover was arriving next week.

The regimental medical officer wrote to Swansea querying their decision, and the Chairman of the DVLC Medical Board, which had made the decision, agreed to refer Robert to a leading expert in brain damage whose rooms were in Harley Street. The appointment was for 11 April and I took Robert in the car.

Parking in Harley Street is always a nightmare and I had to stop double-banked to allow Robert to get out at the door. When he had done so I went off to find a meter and was back at the building in a quarter of an hour. As I entered, Robert was coming out again. He explained what had happened:

'Good morning, young man. Tell me, what has happened to you?'

'Well, sir, I've had a 7.62 high-velocity bullet clean through the head, leaving me with a six-by-two hole in the skull and a severe hemiplegia of the left-hand side of the body, manifesting itself in a totally paralysed left arm, a spastic left ankle and occasional incontinence, but I've had no epilepsy.'

'I see. Thank you.'

The whole examination had taken eight minutes from start to finish.

For the first time since he had been shot, Robert was really depressed and on the point of giving up completely. It was a most distressing sight and made me so angry

that I felt like going back into the building to throttle
this specialist and then getting in my car and driving to
Swansea to sort out the insensitive clowns whose decision
had started it all. Our anger slowly subsided, drowned in
frustration and dejection.

A fortnight went by before the Chairman telephoned
me from Swansea. Apparently the Harley Street specialist
had spoken with the surgeon who had operated on Robert
and both had agreed with a report by a professor at
Glasgow University which said that in all cases like
Robert's there was a thirty to forty per cent chance of
epilepsy occurring within three years of the injury. In these
circumstances, therefore, the Board had decided that
Robert could not drive before 14 June 1984, a generous
decision because that was only two years after he had
been shot.

I told the Chairman that he and his Board were
doing what the Argentinian marines had failed to do on
Tumbledown. They were destroying Robert.

'Well,' he said, 'you can always appeal in a magistrates
court against our decision, and I have to tell you that it is
such an emotive case I believe you would win.'

I suggested that he might take the part of Pontius
Pilate in next year's Passion play. Was he really saying
that his Board's professional decision, based on apparently
erudite medical study, could be overturned by a bench of
lay magistrates?

During the two weeks between Robert's seeing the
Harley Street specialist and my hearing from Swansea
the ban on Robert's driving was uppermost in our minds;
it became a topic of conversation on most occasions. One
such occasion was at the Highland Society of London dinner. I had been a member for only a couple of years and did
not yet know everyone, but the outgoing President's son
had shared a study with Nicholas at school in Edinburgh
and so he always asked about him and his brothers. When
I told him about Robert he immediately introduced me to
the new President, Lord Campbell of Croy. This man had

a kindly face and clearly a genuine interest in other people. I noticed that he was supporting himself by half sitting on the back of a chair which, being very tall, he could do by tilting it just a little. He carried a stick, but it was several minutes before I noticed the callipers on his legs outside the stockings of his Highland dress.

Lord Campbell had been wounded in the spine during the Second World War and after many months in hospital had learned to walk again with the aid of a stick and the callipers. He had led an active political life and had been Secretary of State for Scotland for several years. Throughout his time in Parliament he had taken an active interest in the disabled and he became very interested in Robert.

On 27 April 1983 I wrote to him at the House of Lords: 'When we met at the Highland Society of London dinner on 22 March we discussed the problem of my son Robert, who won the Military Cross with the Scots Guards at Mount Tumbledown and was shot through the head. You may remember that in spite of his astonishing recovery the Driver and Vehicle Licensing Centre at Swansea withdrew his driving licence from 19 March 1983. When we discussed it you invited me to write if I had any problems getting the decision reversed. I very much regret that this is now the case. . . .'

When the Chairman had telephoned from Swansea with his Board's latest decision and suggested that we appeal to a magistrates' court, I had told him I would not bother but instead would appeal to the Minister of Transport. There had been a certain amount of bravado in this, but I had by then already met Lord Campbell of Croy and had also discussed the matter with Sir Hector Monro who was Minister of Sport, the Member for Dumfriesshire and an ex-President of the Scottish Rugby Union. It also crossed my mind that the Home Secretary might be more than a little interested, being a Scots Guardsman himself.

Bravado is very akin to bluff and I have no doubt that the Chairman thought he had called mine when he rang back to say that he had arranged for Robert and me to see Mrs Lynda Chalker, the junior Minister of Transport, on 10 May. It seemed that he was medical adviser to Mrs Chalker and she had readily agreed to see us. I was a little taken aback, but thanked him and assured him that if there were an unsatisfactory outcome we would take his initial advice and go to the magistrates.

That weekend the *Sunday Express* published a very good article under the headline 'Injured hero shock: must not drive'. It was a well-written report, sympathetic but factual and entirely accurate. Lord Campbell had already seen it when my letter arrived, so he had been expecting my cry for help.

His response was to speak to Mrs Chalker and get her to agree to his being present when she saw Robert. He invited us to tea in the House of Lords beforehand, arranging to meet us in the car-park outside. The walk from there into the building was agonizingly slow, giving me time to reflect on the fortunes of these two men, one middle-aged and the other so young, their bodies broken by the ravages of war forty years apart. I wondered if Robert would ever have children and if in another forty years they would also go to war.

Robert needed to find a lavatory after tea so as to be comfortable through the meeting with the Minister. Lord Campbell took him off, leaving me to look round the room, trying to identify the various peers sipping their tea and munching their teacakes. When he came back, Robert was highly amused at having been introduced to the son of a famous field marshal whose main concern had been that Robert's reproductive capabilities should not have been affected by his injury. Robert had reassured him unashamedly and with an enthusiasm that had sent the field marshal's son off roaring with laughter.

The Palace of Westminster is a huge building, and the walk from the House of Lords through endless corridors to the interview room at the side of the Great Hall was another agonizing trek. When we arrived, the doctor from Swansea was already there. He was stoutish and bespectacled and seemed nervous as he introduced himself and the two young civil servants, a woman and a man, who accompanied him. For the next three-quarters of an hour they did not speak, but simply took copious notes.

Lynda Chalker came bustling into the room dead on time yet giving the impression that she was late. She was somewhat matronly in appearance, but looked younger than I had expected. The doctor introduced us and she sat down, took out her glasses and glanced very briefly at her papers. Then, looking Robert straight in the eye, she said, 'Now, Robert, I don't want to stop you driving.'

'Then why are you, Minister?'

'Because I have this report from all these doctors saying that you shouldn't. How many doctors on your Board, Chairman?'

'Seven, Minister.'

'Thank you. Seven doctors, Robert.'

'Really, Minister? How many of them have I met?'

Mrs Chalker turned her head, nodding the question on like a football to the unfortunate doctor.

A grunted reply emerged. 'One, Minister.'

'Oh yes,' said Robert. 'That was the chap I saw in Harley Street for just under ten minutes. He asked me what had happened to me and I told him. I've had a 7.62 high-velocity armour-piercing bullet through the head, sir, leaving me with a six-by-two-inch hole in my skull and a significant hemiplegia of the left-hand side of my body which manifests itself in a paralysed left arm, a spastic left ankle and a certain amount of incontinence, but I have had no epilepsy. Now what did he say about me to you?'

The doctor blinked behind his glasses and cleared his throat as he fumbled with the papers in his file.

'Ah yes, here it is,' he said at last. 'This young man has received a high-velocity bullet through the head leaving him with a six-by-two-inch hole in the skull and a significant hemiplegia of the left-hand side of his body which manifests itself in a paralysed left arm, a spastic left ankle and a certain amount of incontinence. He has had no epilepsy.'

His voice trailed off as he realized he was reading what Robert had just said, and we could hardly hear the final phrase. He looked at Robert and we all followed his gaze. Robert was grinning.

'I know that by heart now, Minister.'

Lynda Chalker looked at me and then quickly turned back to Robert.

'You seem to have made a point, Robert. Nevertheless we do have this very deep study by Professor Jinnet of Glasgow University based on every head wound suffered in the First and Second World Wars, Malaya, Korea, Borneo, Vietnam, Northern Ireland, you name it, and it suggests there is a thirty to forty per cent chance of epilepsy occurring within three years of the injury. This is why the Board at Swansea felt it necessary to ban you from driving. Now they have revised their original decision and have said you can drive in June 1984 provided you do not have a fit before then. In the meantime I am prepared to authorize a chauffeur-driven car for your use. How would that be for you?'

'That's very kind,' Robert replied, 'but a chauffeur wouldn't want to keep my hours and in any case I do not accept the Board's decision. None of them has seen me. This gentleman even asked my father if we needed a wheelchair for today. None of them bothered to find out about me. All right, I accept the professor's study and his statistics, but only if you can tell me that every case with which he has compared me was that of a twenty-one-year-old at the peak of physical fitness, hit from behind by a 7.62 high-velocity bullet at nine hundred feet above sea-level and fifty-two degrees latitude south and a temperature below freezing point — or were some of them perhaps older, less fit, hit by a .5 or .303 low-velocity bullet from in front or the side, at sea-level or in the desert or in the jungle? If they were all like me, then I accept your statistics, but even so, what does a thirty to

rty per cent chance mean? Presumably it covers the full
venty-four hours, but for how many of them am I likely
be in my car during the day? Surely the real figure is
ore like a five per cent chance.'

The doctor shifted uneasily in his seat and the Minister
ared at her papers.

'I am sorry, Robert, I have a responsibility to other
embers of the public.'

'Responsibility?' he said. 'Oh, I know about responsibil-
y; I had responsibility on Tumbledown Mountain. Do you
ink we'd have taken it if through a sense of responsibility
had decided not to attack as we did?'

For the first time since we had sat down I inter-
ened.

'May I suggest, Minister, that the crux of the matter
that statistically Robert is dead and so we need not be
ere.'

'Yes, I take your point,' she said. Then, after a short
ause, she continued. 'Robert, I'll tell you what I am
repared to do. You can see three doctors — suitable
pecialists, that is — of your own choice and if they
ecommend that you be allowed to drive, so be it,
nd if not then my offer of a car and chauffeur stands.
ord Campbell, you can probably help with finding three
uitable specialists.'

His Lordship said he certainly could and would be very
leased to do so.

The Minister stood up, shook hands with Robert, me and
ord Campbell and, as she left the room, once again giving
he impression that she was late, said, 'I only hope Hector
nd the Home Secretary are happy with that. You've no
dea how much pressure I've had put on me about you,
obert.'

He grinned as he thanked her and she really looked quite
leased with herself.

On the way home I wondered what would have hap-
ened if Robert had been, say, an able seaman whose
ather was a bus driver from Leeds, or if he had been a

gunner with no relatives at all except perhaps a widowe
mother. People in such circumstances might have strug
gled. Of course Robert was an officer, not an able seama
or a gunner, and under no circumstances would he hav
taken all this lying down, even if he had not had the benef
of my experience and contacts. In effect I had got us th
interview and had lined up a bit of heavy artillery, but
was Robert who did the talking when it mattered and h
who carried the day. Again the irony of it all struck me. O
the one hand, if he were not the person he is, he would n
have got shot and would not have won the Military Cros
on the other hand, if he were not the person he is and y
had still been shot, he would probably not have survive
let alone overcome the injury.

* * *

True to his word, Lord Campbell arranged for thre
neuro-surgeons, all acceptable to Swansea, to see Rober
who was due to have his final operation in July durin
which the hole in his head would be closed with acryli
They all agreed there was no need to stop him driving an
that to do so would do untold damage psychologically. On
surgeon thought it might be wise to wait until after th
operation, but he did not press the point, and one year t
the day after being shot Robert received his new licenc
and was at last mobile again.

The Rover was an excellent car with everything h
needed — automatic gear transmission, power-assiste
steering, and light and indicator switches adapted t
enable him to drive with the right hand only. It wa
a solid, well-built car which was unlikely to crumple o
collapse around him if by any chance he hit anything
However, although he himself had originally chosen i
from the stipulated British Leyland range, he soon cam
to realize it was not a young man's car. Why coul
he not have a fun car? Something in which he coul
take out his girlfriend and look the part in spite o
having only half a body. It worried me that he was s

discontent. We had so much to be thankful for. Could he not see that?

'I am not driving that hearse any more. Do you know what someone shouted from outside the Antelope as I drove past yesterday evening? Go careful with Daddy's car, sonny!'

He was hurt and angry. Instinctively he had stopped to demonstrate, but Tanya had restrained him and had got out herself to deliver a five-foot verbal roasting that left the group outside the pub apologetic and ashamed.

It did not help. In fact if anything it made matters worse for Robert to have his girlfriend fighting his battles for him. Perhaps if she had been on Tumbledown she would have done a better job than he without getting herself shot.

Ten days after that incident and six months after he had taken delivery of the Rover, we were being shown brochures of a British racing green Panther Kallista, hand-built at Byfleet near the pre-war Brooklands race track. It would mean losing five thousand pounds on the Rover, but it would be worth it. Everything was being adapted to meet Robert's needs and there was no doubt that it was going to be the answer to all Robert had ever wanted. Nick, his brother, was the car expert and he was very impressed, so we should be too.

Within a few weeks we were summoned to the White Swan, a pub on the river at Twickenham, for a Saturday lunch-time drink. It was Nick's particular haunt and the place was packed with his friends. Melanie shepherded Jean into a corner, and I had a pint thrust into my hand within seconds of arriving.

'Where's Robert?' I asked.

'Oh, he'll be here in a minute. He's picking up his new girlfriend.'

I could not believe it. A new girlfriend? Tanya was such a sweet girl, so loving, so kind and so attractive.

Nick's grin confirmed it nevertheless.

'She shouldn't have fought his battles,' he said. 'From what I hear, this one won't know how to.'

A throaty engine revved up outside and all head
turned. We went outside and there it stood on th
road by the river bank. The sleek bonnet was twic
as long as the rest of the car. The hood was down, c
course, and in the cockpit — for that was what it seeme
like to me — Robert sat smiling, debonair and totally i
control of the situation. Beside him sat the girl from th
chocolates advertisement. She had gorgeous eyes, and a
she opened the door and gingerly placed one shapely foc
on the road, the rest of her beauty slowly unfolded befor
the admiring crowd. Nick was first to the Panther, closel
followed by Chris. They both ignored the girl and went t
their brother's side. He looked up grinning as they ben
over him, laughing and joking, examining every dial, ever
switch. The sophisticated stereo boomed out the lates
rock tape and gradually the car was surrounded by th
crowd. Robert struggled out of the driving seat and cast
quick glance across to the girl.

She was long-legged and very beautiful, and I marvelle
quietly to myself that Robert was still able to attract sucl
a cracker. Jean and I were standing at the top of the step
and he waved as he caught sight of us. Melanie joined u
and asked if we had met the lovely Bea. We said we ha
not and were led forward to be introduced. Jean was take
up first, while I was diverted to the other side of the car b
Robert.

'What do you think, Daddy?'

'Great,' I said, 'and the car's not bad either!'

He laughed and I reassured him that the Panthe
was fantastic. As for the girl, she was Belgian, thoug
she had been educated in England, and she was calle
either Beatrice or Beatrix — he really wasn't sure, bu
Bea would do.

Thinking about it on the way home, I realized tha
fantastic was exactly the right word to describe the car
As someone at the pub had said, 'That's not a car, it'
a statement.' With it, Robert could once again be th
dashing young officer, even the wounded hero, but withou

it he was nothing, broken, weak, immobile, crippled.

'Never trust a cripple,' my father-in-law used to say. It was not a phrase I had ever liked, and I had always had difficulty understanding it. I wondered whether, if he had still been alive, he would have trusted his grandson now he was a cripple. My father-in-law had lied about his age in the First World War and at seventeen had been in the first gas attack. After wandering for three days half blind in the mud of no man's land, he had stumbled back through his own lines. A year in St George's Hospital had then seen him discharged to a likely death before he reached the age of twenty, but like Robert he had cheated and had lived, to work, marry and produce a daughter and, through her, another wounded soldier. He had eventually died at the age of fifty-nine, suffering a heart attack at the wheel of his car in North Shields High Street. Robert never knew his maternal grandfather, but all through school and ever since he has had his bayonet on the wall of his room, a bayonet carried through the Somme, twice the length but only half as sharp as the one Robert himself carried up Tumbledown.

When first discharged, Robert's grandfather had been given a silver badge bearing the inscription 'For loyalty' to help him ward off patriotic women wielding white feathers. He had received a small pension, but this was stopped when he got his first job. The British Legion offered to fight to get it back, but he had had enough of fighting. He wanted to get on and enjoy life. He had cheated death once, but might not manage it when it came a second time, like tomorrow.

I wondered how long Robert would go on cheating death.

DISCHARGED FROM
THE ARMY

John Lawrence

In July Robert went into hospital again to have the missing bone in his skull replaced with a special acrylic substance. Robert gave me a lump of it to use as a paperweight and I marvelled at the hardness of it — a cross between stone and bone.

Seeing the nine-inch scar again, jagged and black through the shaved stubble of his head, brought back memories of that awful day at RAF Wroughton when he had first come back from Montevideo. There was swelling all around the scar and he was convinced the surgeon had made a mess of it by putting in too much acrylic plastic. It distressed his mother greatly also and they both clearly thought he would go around for the rest of his life with a grotesque, misshapen head. I found this faintly hysterical and was only thankful that the operation had been successful.

The hospital suggested that Robert come to us for a few days when he was discharged, but he declined and insisted on returning to his flat.

Jean and I then went for a short holiday to Sark in the Channel Islands. It was idyllic and as always a week was not long enough, but we benefited and came back refreshed.

As usual, the first thing we did was to contact Robert. He said he was fine, but I knew something was wrong. We went round to the flat and sure enough he had received a letter from the Ministry of Defence.

Sir

1. I am directed to inform you that your Short Service Commission was due to end on 3 August 1983, but owing to an administrative error you were not informed that your terminal leave should have started on 7 July 1983. It has now been decided that you will be transferred to the Reserve on 19 September 1983.

2. The requisite notification will appear in the London Gazette (Supplement) on or about 20 September 1983.

3. I am to conclude by taking this opportunity of thanking you for your services while on the Active List.

I am, Sir,
Your obedient Servant

I just could not believe my eyes. He was being discharged as a short-service officer, possibly with a gratuity, but with no guarantee of a pension let alone knowledge of how much it would be and apparently without even a release medical to confirm he was fit enough for discharge.

Robert Lawrence

I was absolutely stunned by the letter. For a start, whoever sent it would surely have thought, here is a rarity, a lieutenant with a Military Cross — I wonder what the circumstances are? They obviously did not, but even more crucial was this ludicrous notion of my being placed on the Reserve — recalled to the next war in a wheelchair! It just emphasized again how unimportant the system considered me to be.

My father hit the roof, and sent off a formal letter to the Adjutant General to get this state of affairs adjusted. We had only three weeks to sort things out, because once I was discharged from the Army we would be faced with fighting the whole amorphous might of the Department of Social Security.

Three days later the Adjutant General replied. His letter

confirmed the withdrawal of the previous one informing me of my discharge. Secondly, it said that a full medical examination would be arranged which would determine, in an indirect way, the level of my pension, if any. It went on to explain that the Army medical board would prepare a report, which would go to the Department of Health and Social Security, who in turn would convene a medical board, which would then assess the level of my disability. Unfortunately, this would happen only once I had left the Army.

The next letter I got informed me that my short-service gratuity would be £4,158. It was stereo-typed with the figures entered in ink and began 'Dear Sir/Madam'. Yet another example of the workings of a thoughtless bureaucratic system. And yet another occasion when my father felt obliged to hit the roof.

In October I received another letter which said:

Sir

1. I am directed to inform you that, as the Medical Board by which you were examined on 12 September 1983 pronounced you as unfit for any form of military service under existing standards your retirement an account of disability will be carried out with effect from 14 November 1983.
2. The requisite notification will appear in the London Gazette (Supplement) on or about 15 November 1983.
3. You will be informed about terminal benefits by the Army Pensions Office in due course. The address of the Army Pensions Office is 103-109 Waterloo Street, Glasgow G2 7BN.
4. I am to inform you that the Secretary of State for Defence has it in command from The Queen to convey to you, on your leaving the Active List of the Army, the thanks of Her Majesty for your valuable services.

I am, Sir,
Your obedient Servant

When I received the first letter informing me of my discharge from the Army, I returned to Chelsea Barracks to say goodbye to my old platoon. I went into the company commander's office, and there sat a new company commander whom I didn't know very well — my previous company commander having moved on.

'Hello, Robert,' he said. 'What are you doing here?'

'Well, I'm being discharged from the Army now,' I replied, 'and I've come to say goodbye to my platoon.'

He looked up briefly. 'You know, I don't think it's very good for morale for the boys to see you limping around the barracks like this. So if I were you, Robert, I'd hurry up and get out of camp.'

I couldn't say anything. I was disgusted and extremely hurt, and also there was still this residual influence of my Army training holding me back. This guy was a major and I was a lieutenant and I simply couldn't turn round and bawl him out. Recently my wife and I enjoyed enormously a private party given by that now retired major.

Once I'd left the Army, no one ever rang me up to see how I was, or to ask me whether they could help me with my career, as they'd always suggested they would do as 'the family'. They never asked whether I was getting better or whether I was getting worse. So much for the buddy-buddy, pally-pally regiment, the Army that demands so much from its men in incredibly long hours and great personal sacrifice. Loyalty, as far as the Army was concerned, seemed a pretty one-way street to me.

CIVILIAN LIFE

John Lawrence

We read the last letter from the Ministry of Defence several times. At least it now stated that Robert was medically unfit and also referred to his 'retirement on account of disability'. These seemed to me to be two crucial factors and the fact that it gave the address of the Army Pensions Office was encouraging too, though we still did not know how much pension he would get.

The other pleasing aspect of the letter was the wording of the thanks. 'The Secretary of State for Defence has in command from The Queen to convey to you, on your leaving the Active List of the Army, the thanks of Her Majesty for your valuable services.' There was dignity and a source of pride in that, so much more than in some anonymous civil servant's confessing to having made an administrative error and then 'taking this opportunity to thank you for your services while on the Active List'.

Slowly Robert began to accept that it was over. He even made enquiries about resettlement courses, and the battalion second-in-command gave him some examples of curricula vitae which he had himself learned to write on such a course.

Robert joined a business orientation course whose instructor was an ex-Gurkha officer who had walked out of the jungle after escaping from the Japanese in the Second World War. He had written a book about it and gave Robert a copy. In the front he wrote a very moving inscription 'from one wounded junior officer to another'. He had been in the XIVth Army, which had been known as the 'Forgotten Army'.

When I read that inscription I wondered if he was suggesting that Robert was to be a forgotten hero. How could anyone forget what my youngest son had done? Then I quickly realized that the majority of people would soon forget the Falklands. War and its aftermath were far too unpleasant and embarrassing, they were best forgotten and erased from the mind as soon as possible.

Robert's views on the subject were very clear. He had done his job as a professional soldier as well as he could and had been unlucky enough to be hit. That was tough and he accepted it without bitterness. But he was disillusioned by the Army's apparent lack of interest in him, and he was also upset by the way the public seemed just to take it all for granted. During the war and for a few weeks afterwards there was much flag-waving and drum-beating, but it soon subsided. We had won, but what did you expect? Of course we had won, and won well. It was in fact brilliantly done, over a vast eight thousand miles' distance, but supposing we had lost? Some say we were down to one shell per gun, and there was no doubt in Robert's mind that if the Scots Guards had not taken Tumbledown Mountain, the Argentinians could have counter-attacked out of Port Stanley and driven them back to San Carlos Bay — not only Scots Guards but Marines and bloody Paras as well. Then where would we have been? The Dunkirk spirit would not have been a lot of use and the Great might have gone out of Great Britain for ever.

He was distressed by the rapid loss of interest and the apparent lack of appreciation.

'One hundred years ago I'd have been set up for life with a good pension and a sinecure job. Today I am an embarrassment. No one knows what to do with wounded officers.'

I too was distressed. Whatever happened, I did not want him to turn resentful or bitter. Although I sympathized with his views, I could not accept them entirely. His pension would be sorted out eventually and I was fairly sure the regiment would find him a job if necessary,

though I knew he did not want that. I recalled a verse from
Robert Burns's 'Jolly Beggars' about the soldier who los
a leg on the Heights of Abraham. No one bothered abou
him either. Robert's own platoon song 'I will go' has a la
verse also about soldiers returning from the war.

> When we came back to the glen
> Winter was turning
> Our goods lay in the snow
> And our houses were burning
> I will go, I will go.

By comparison Robert was very fortunate, and he ha
much to be thankful for, but he was not yet ready fo
that argument. The problem was one of frustration. H
always wanted to get on with the next task — tomorrov
was never soon enough, and next year an eternity away.

Almost six weeks after his discharge date his pensio
was finally settled. It had taken a number of telephon
calls to various parts of the widely spread Department o
Health and Social Security before we eventually tracke
down a very helpful lady in an office at Norcross, nea
Blackpool, who took pity and, more importantly, a per
sonal interest.

Robert was assessed as one hundred per cent disable
and accordingly would get a tax-free war pension, subjec
to review, for the rest of his life. The rate was sufficientl
generous to mean that he would never actually starve
Some of his friends at first thought it very generous, bu
after reflection most of them agreed that they would no
have wanted to give what Robert had given to be paid a
a retired junior captain for the rest of their lives with n
prospect of promotion whatsoever. The South Atlanti
Fund had also been generous and Robert therefore ha
money to invest. Even so, Jean in particular was quit
upset that not all the money given to the Fund by th
public was distributed to victims of the Falklands War. I
was reported that several millions of pounds were allotte

to each of the three service charities, including the RAF
Benevolent Fund. As far as I know there was only one
RAF casualty in the Falklands War, the pilot who had
been at Headley Court with Robert. To give the RAF Fund
as much as the other two service funds therefore seemed
strange.

Two aspects of life particularly concerned Robert. First,
the general administration of his affairs presented an
enormous burden. Jean and I did all we could, and his
brothers also helped to a degree, but we all had our
own lives to lead and in any case tended to suggest ways
of doing things that were not as he wanted. The lady
caretaker of the building where Robert had his flat lived in
the next-door basement, and she had taken him under her
wing as far as cleaning his flat was concerned and also in
terms of keeping a general eye on things, but she could in
no way act as secretary or personal assistant. Until he was
actually discharged from the Army he still had Hamilton,
his Guardsman orderly, who came round three or four
times a week. He worshipped Robert, but had to confine
himself to cleaning his shoes and brushing his suits. From
19 November he could no longer come during working
hours and in December he was posted away to Cyprus.

Robert Lawrence

Having the use of only one arm and one leg brings
a lot of complications. Even the most ridiculously little
things are difficult. You have to learn to do up shoes
one-handed, open bottles and cans one-handed, cut bread
one-handed. You cannot do up your right shirt cuff, and
if you pull up one side of a pair of trousers, the other
side stays down. I managed to overcome these problems,
but only after the most laborious mental application and
patience. Each morning to roll up my right sleeve I must
put the shirt on back to front, roll up the sleeve on
my bad arm and then, putting the shirt on the right

way round, repeat the process to have both sleeves rolled up.

I now had to try and work out what I was going to do with the rest of my life. I believed I'd been extremely well-trained in logistics and man management, aspects of Army work that I could still put to use elsewhere. Obviously there wasn't going to be much call for a disabled jungle warfare instructor in civilian life. So instead I would have to focus not only on something that would suit me, my character and what I had learned in the past, but also on something that could accommodate my injury.

Through Tanya, I had met many very intelligent and creative people, artists, actors and so on, with whom I felt I had a lot in common. They were all struggling to get on in their various fields, and meeting them increased my own desire, which had by then been growing for some time, to go into the media and entertainment industry. I felt that, like the Army, it was an area with the potential for people to do the things that mattered. If you wrote the right kind of book, for instance, or made the right sort of documentary, it might actually affect people's lives. Films, in particular, would also demand the sort of skills in logistics and people management I mentioned before; setting them up was practically an Army-type operation.

I was a military man, with the bearing of such, and initially I think a lot of Tanya's drama-school friends saw me as some sort of narrow-minded fascist. Of course, one could argue that it was pretty narrow-minded of arts people, in turn, to categorize all military people in that way but, bizarrely perhaps, once they discovered that I had actually done a proper soldier's job of fighting and killing and getting wounded, they tended to be more lenient with me.

Before I finally left the Army, I worked briefly for Production Partners, a firm that made television commercials. I had been introduced to them by an incredible man called Jimmy Wright, who had been an RAF reconnaissance pilot during the last war, taking films and aerial photographs of enemy territory. During this time he had been shot down, extremely badly burned and had to have his face completely reconstructed with plastic surgery. He had also been blinded for life, but was determined to carry on in the film industry, as he had been a cameraman before the war. I offered my services to his company, in Soho, free, just to get some experience. I worked basically as a 'runner', a dogsbody who runs errands and makes the coffee. I couldn't have been a very efficient 'runner', as such, with my disability, but I tried to make up for a shortfall in the running area by helping in other ways.

The film people I met through Production Partners seemed friendly to a remarkable degree. I remember once asking a lighting man in a Soho pub why this should be and he said, 'What you have got to understand, Robert, is that although you may be only twenty-two or twenty-three now, some day you may want to employ one of us. Most people in this business are free-lance, and one day you could become a producer. So *of course* we are going to be nice.'

The time in Soho taught me a lot, and helped me down the road to improving my image. And in Guildford, while still on Army sick leave, I decided to build on that and spend some time working at the Yvonne Arnaud Theatre.

On leaving the Army, I was given a list of possible courses I could take and, following my film and theatre experience, I decided I needed to improve my business acumen. At the back of my mind was the idea that if, as I hoped, I was eventually going to become a producer, then I should know more about how the City worked. It might prove a future source of financial backing.

In late 1983 I began a business appreciation course at the Central London Polytechnic. There were about twenty to thirty people on it, most of whom were twice my age and over, but it was high-powered and I learned a lot. The tutor in charge was an ex-Army lieutenant called Ian MacHorton. He had been in the Chindits in Burma, and had been injured fighting out there, which led to a great empathy being established between us. It was helpful and encouraging for me to meet someone else who had been hurt in the past, yet who had still gone on to be a very successful businessman. One day he presented me with a book he had written about his life, signed with the following message:

> To Robert,
> From one wounded junior officer to another, as we and only we can understand the problems involved. From my luck draw the strength to further your own luck. We will win. Congratulations on your track record.
> With best wishes in Our Hearts,
> Ian.

It inspired hope, of course, but I still seemed to have a long way to go.

From the minute I left the Army, and certainly throughout the London business course, like most young Guards officers I received various vague offers of jobs in the City. Eventually, through my elder brother Chris, who, after leaving the Army had himself become a stockbroker, I was offered a job at Northcote and Co., a small stockbroking firm in the City.

Basically what they said to me was, this is the training course. You will spend X number of months in this department, X number of months in that department, you'll do this, then you'll do that, and eventually you will become a stockbroker. The problem was, that was not my aim. My aim was to find out as much as I could that would benefit a future career in television and films. I explained this to them, and offered to work for them for no salary, just to learn a bit, as by now my Army pension was coming in. Very kindly they agreed to this.

John Lawrence

Although Army life is varied, it has an ordered routine and Robert was used not only to that, but also to discipline, especially self-discipline. 'Them what's keen gets fell-in early' was an old family maxim.

For his first few weeks at Northcote Robert was seldom early, but he was always on time. Christopher's friends at the firm, whom I also knew, told me that not only was Robert punctual, his turn-out was always immaculate — smart suit, stiff collar, silk spotted tie or perhaps the dark red and blue stripes of the brigade tie. Of course Robert would correct that description. It was no longer the Brigade of Guards, but the Household Division. He may have been capable of being a rebel but he could also be a stickler for accuracy and detail. I learned later that in order to arrive at the office on time and dressed in that fashion he rose at six o'clock every morning.

City life has its hazards, not least working lunches and relaxing evenings. In consequence my fears about his social life were soon compounded by thoughts of his burning the candle at both ends and in the middle as well. I suggested that he should be careful and throttle back, but I need not have worried. Robert was not a survivor for nothing. Discreet enquiries revealed that he was in fact pacing himself quite well. He was seldom getting involved in lunch-time appointments and was frequently dropping out of evening engagements. When he did go out to lunch it was specifically to meet theatre contacts who might be useful if he did manage to go into a career in production.

I was relieved by this, but staying in during the evenings did not please his girlfriend. She was young and energetic and loved having a good time. Little conflicts arose, and Robert's innate chauvinism sometimes came to the surface, but they never lasted very long and he quite often gave way in the end.

Quite why he did not stick with stockbroking longer than he did is difficult to say. It may be that the rebel inside him asserted itself and he decided he did not accept the conventions of City hours and City dress. He loved looking smart, and in fact could be quite a popinjay at times, but he wanted the freedom to dress as he wanted, when he wanted. Several times at a birthday party or some other celebration where most people were in corduroys or jeans he would turn up in his white tuxedo dinner jacket. On other occasions he would love to shock by appearing in bomber jacket, jeans, basketball boots and a black and white checked PLO *khafiyah*. Fortunately he had the sense to wear it round his neck and not as a head-dress.

In addition to this aspect of City life, he probably found the hours and the type of concentration too much to cope with. For whatever reason, he eventually left the firm.

There was complete understanding by all and he left with the good wishes of everybody in the office.

Robert Lawrence

During my time at Northcote, besides learning a lot about money and investments, I wrote to every single contact I could find in the theatre industry. I thought it might be easier initially to get into than the film industry, and it led to my meeting some very interesting and helpful people.

I remember one day having lunch at the Garrick Club with Derek Nimmo — whom I had met before, at the Leyland car launch — when the Queen Mother arrived, along with some Jockey Club guests. Having recognized Derek and his other guest, actor William Fox — who was downing some bizarre green cocktail called Tarts Tickles — she came across and joined us for a drink. She was great company and took delight, I recall, in entering a cordoned-off area of the club that had previously always been restricted to men only. There were cheers all round.

Several lunches later, I was advised to go and see Ray Cooney, who runs the Theatre of Comedy, quite a big theatre production company which owns the Shaftesbury Theatre and the Ambassadors Theatre in London. Up in the gods at the Shaftesbury, I had a long chat with Ray about what I was trying to do, and he put me in touch with another powerful character in the theatrical world, Thelma Holt: strong, red-haired, outspoken, fairly left-wing — and not afraid of anybody.

'I'm Robert Lawrence,' I told her on introduction, after waiting several weeks for an appointment. 'Ray Cooney will have told you all about me.'

'I know absolutely nothing about you at all,' she said. 'Tell me.'

By this stage I had learned a little about self-presentation. I knew that if you were dealing with a staunchly right-wing Conservative, you would have to portray the image of a sincere young man, an ex-Guards officer, who had fought for your country, won the Military Cross, and so on. If you were dealing with a person with more left-wing tendencies, who tended not to approve of militarism and patriotism, then you were a hard-done-by injured victim of capitalist oppression. Such is the world we live in.

Through Thelma, with whom I eventually got on very well, I ended up working as assistant to the director on productions at the Ambassadors Theatre, for sixty pounds a week. Between productions I used to work in the theatre's office, for nothing, in order to get a place on the next production. On one production, *Top People*, I was personal assistant to Richard O'Brien, its director, who had also created the *Rocky Horror Show*.

Around that time, about May 1984, I moved from Sloane Square to a house in Clapham, and Richard was one of the guests I asked along to my drinks party to celebrate. He is tall, very, very skinny and a quite outrageous, marvellous character. The sight of him with his shaved head and tight jeans chatting merrily to my father on this occasion seemed to beg a photograph.

When I showed this to my father afterwards, he was amused and said, 'If you'd shown me a picture of myself talking to a man who looked like that two years earlier, I just wouldn't have believed it.' It was yet another occasion when I was to see his old ideals and restrictions being broken down.

THE BATTLE CONTINUES

John Lawrence

I still had hopes of physical improvement for Robert. The doctors had said it could happen anything up to three years after his receiving the wound and I continued to cling to the idea that if medical science advanced as far in the next thirty years as it had in the last thirty, someone would invent an implant that could replace the missing part of his brain and get his arm and leg working again. In thirty years' time he would be only my age and hopefully still have time to enjoy life.

Such thoughts were nevertheless tinged with others about the transitory nature of life. Who can tell when we will die? All we can say is that we certainly will die one day. Robert could not understand why he was not dead already and when his grandmother suggested he had been saved for a purpose, he asked fervently that someone please tell him what it was because he had to get on and do it now — not tomorrow or in thirty years' time, but now.

Although we had seen the scar across his shaved head when Robert first came home and again after the operation in the Maudsley Hospital, and although we could see the external effects of his injury, it was difficult to imagine the pain and anguish it caused him. He had told us how much blood he had lost, but even though I knew that there were eight pints in the whole body and therefore that he had lost more than half, the full significance of the statistic was hard to grasp, other than to think that he should have died.

I received a letter from a doctor at St George's Hospital, Tooting, inviting me to a lecture to be given by an Army medical officer who had been in charge of the field hospitals in the Falklands. He had heard of Robert's injury and thought I might be interested in attending.

When I arrived I was shown into a lecture room with a number of others, men and women, most of whom appeared to be members of the medical profession. I was not introduced to the lecturer until afterwards, when I was a little taken aback to learn that he had known I was in the audience.

Lieutenant-Colonel Roberts had commanded the Field Ambulance Unit which had done such amazing work during the Falklands campaign. He had also put together an excellent photographic record of their work from the training period in Wales, through the voyage south and the war, to the triumphant return home. He talked about the deployment of his units and how he had deliberately changed the standard organization to meet the particular requirements of the task facing them in the Falklands. All through the talk he showed slide after coloured slide, many of them outstanding photographs.

After half an hour I was getting a little bored with the proceedings, but then he showed a slide of the refrigeration plant at Ajax Bay, where the main field hospital had been, and others of the forward posts at Teal Inlet and Fitzroy. I began to take an interest again. Fitzroy was near Bluff Cove and had been used to deal initially with the burned Welsh Guards from the *Sir Galahad*. It was also the nearest post to Tumbledown and the one to which Robert had been taken.

The picture on the screen left a lasting impression of a dark shed with just one solitary light bulb hanging from the ceiling over a makeshift operating table, probably made from a door and two packaging cases. It was like a scene from the television comedy programme set in the Korean war, *M*A*S*H*.

The screen went blank and the light from it showed up the lecturer who explained that one of their biggest problems, apart from burns, had been dealing with high-velocity bullet wounds. I listened intently. He explained how the speed of the bullet sets up a shock wave which removes most things in its way. He had some slides to illustrate this, but they were fairly gory and he advised anyone of a squeamish disposition not to look. I glanced furtively round the room, but saw no one drop their eyes or turn away. My own gaze was drawn back to the screen as the automatic changer clicked and the next picture appeared.

'This shows the effect of a high-velocity bullet through the fleshy part of a thigh. As you can see, the 7.62-millimetre bullet has passed straight through the leg, but the shock wave it sets up has left a furrow through the flesh about ten or twelve centimetres wide.'

I remained riveted to the screen as the next slide came up. This one was of a similar wound in the upper arm, but because of the lesser thickness of the limb and the shattering of the bone it was a great deal more messy than the one in the first slide.

'Having seen what happens to flesh and bones in the limbs, can you imagine what it does to the head? Yet miraculously we had one young officer shot through the head with a high-velocity bullet and he survived. In fact he never lost consciousness and gave us a really hard time because the surgeons took so long to get to him. The truth was, of course, that they gave him no chance and worked only on those they thought they could save. In the event, we never had any die on us once we got them to Fitzroy, Teal Inlet or Ajax Bay.'

When the lecture finished I was introduced to Colonel Roberts. He explained that he had known I was in the audience and so had deliberately not shown the slides of Robert. There were three in all and if I would like to have copies I was very welcome to them. I declined the offer, but said I would ask Robert if he wanted them. When I telephoned him he could not wait to see them. It took me a few weeks to track down the Colonel and get

them sent, and when they arrived I could hardly believe
my eyes. They were indescribably horrific, with blood and
surgical instruments everywhere, the first picture showing
the wide open wound and the last showing it sewn up.
The angles from which they had been taken were such
that Robert's face was plainly recognizable in all three
photographs.

I hesitated to show them to Jean, but at her insistence
did so eventually. She was close to being sick, but being
Jean she was not. Robert thought they were marvellous.
At last he could believe the miracle of his survival. We
got another set printed and for several years he carried
them in his wallet, producing them at every opportunity,
almost enjoying the shock they brought to people, at
least in the early days. After a while he became more
circumspect and showed them to girls and women only if
they absolutely insisted, as his mother had done with me.
I have a feeling that in several cases insistence brought on
a lack of resistance and he was able to take full advantage,
in the nicest possible way, of course, of the sympathy thus
engendered.

He showed them to Beatrice, but she was so shocked
she told him never to show them to her again.

Their relationship seemed to be deepening, and Jean
and I were pleased for him that once again he had found
a caring and attractive girl who was apparently prepared
to accept him as he was. This was very comforting, but I
wondered all the time how long it would last. She was very
young, good-looking and wealthy. At least, her father was
very wealthy, with houses in Belgium, Paris and London.
Her elder sister was studying in England and seemed to be
more favoured, especially by her father. Robert tried to
avoid entanglement in their family disputes, but inevitably
was occasionally drawn into taking Beatrice's part against
either her sister or one of her parents.

As they saw more and more of each other, so Robert
got involved with Beatrice's schoolfriends, most of whom
were from similarly wealthy families. He had plenty of his

own friends as well, of course, and between the two he was soon plunged into a hectic social whirl of charity balls, nights out at Annabel's nightclub and wining and dining; he was known to the head waiters of most half-decent restaurants in London.

It was undoubtedly great fun and he deserved to have some, but it worried me on two counts. First, it was very expensive, and secondly, I wondered about the physical strain on his mind and body. He had lost weight and his left side was wasting visibly. Sleeping was not always easy and he still had nightmares, during which he wrecked the bed, if not the room.

The problem of incontinence was also still with him, not often, admittedly, but it was totally unpredictable. On one occasion he had to abandon the Panther in the middle of the West End and make for a nearby hotel. This entailed crossing the road and in his hurry he stumbled on the kerb of a traffic island and fell. When he hit the ground his bowels emptied and he lay there in the road struggling to get up, needing help yet fearful that someone would come to assist him and be repelled by his condition. The wasted side made it difficult, but he was learning new tricks every day and the dread of someone's approaching him spurred him on. With the help of first the kerb and then the bollard on the island he dragged himself back on to his feet and regained the sanctuary of his car. Once there he composed himself a little before roaring off through the traffic, foul and angry, back to his flat. Had he been stopped by an over-zealous policeman the chances are that he would have dropped his trousers to prove his point and been charged with indencency as well as speeding. As it was, he got home without further mishap, phoned his mother, put his soiled clothes in a plastic bag and climbed into a hot bath where she found him apologetic but fairly cheerful half an hour later.

There seemed to be no limit to his resilience, but even the deepest well needs replenishment and it was difficult to see from where this would come. He could not go on living by continually raising the bucket and tipping it over himself either to cleanse or to revive. One day the well must surely run dry.

Robert Lawrence

My new career may have been making some progress, but coming to terms with all the different aspects of my disability remained a constant battle. Often, I would still have the most terrible nightmares, and on one distressing occasion I beat up a girlfriend in my sleep.

One morning I woke up in excruciating pain and discovered that I couldn't move at all. I have two fused vertebrae in my neck caused by whiplash from the Falklands bullet, and with the terror brought on by a bad dream during the night, they had simply frozen in position, causing the neck muscles to go into spasm. With great difficulty, I eventually managed to get myself out of bed to ring my father. It must have been about five o'clock in the morning, but he came straight over in his car to Clapham, with a spare set of keys to the house.

When he found me, I had managed to get back to my bed from the telephone but I hadn't been able to get into it. I was simply sitting there, on the edge of it, freezing cold and unable to move. The slightest movement was agony, and in the end my father had to take me to a private osteopath to get the problem sorted out.

From time to time, incidents would occur that would tip my already fragile mental state over the edge, such as the time my prized Panther Kallista car was broken into and vandalized. This was not the first time it had happened; in fact, the Panther had been vandalized several times while I was living in Clapham, which I found very frustrating and hurtful. This particular morning, I had got up especially early to go to an antiques fair — something I've always enjoyed doing — and when I found the car wrecked yet again, and its stereo system ripped out in the process, it was just too much. I absolutely freaked, kicking the hell out of all the parked cars that were hemming the Panther in and smashing hell out of the Panther as well, before erupting into general hysterics and tears.

Beatrice, my girlfriend at the time, finally got me into the car and drove me to my parents. I was as near to totally cracking up as anybody could be, and my mother arranged that I go away with her to Shrublands Hall, a health farm in Suffolk, for several weeks to get over it. Beatrice had been terrified by the whole incident, and I had to find somewhere where I could blow off steam.

Following this, there was a happy period, but then I broke up with Beatrice, and was thrown back into gloom.

Beatrice was about the most beautiful girl I had ever seen, but very young, nineteen or so, when I started going out with her. Her father, a Belgian and probably the most conspicuously wealthy man I have ever met, did not approve of her association with me. Had I been a good little rich boy, working in the City, he probably would have liked me more, I don't know. But I got the feeling he was also unhappy about my disability, and in particular about the fact that I suffered from incontinence.

The fact is that owing to the paralysis I have a weak bowel and a weak bladder, and from time to time in the first year or so of my injury, especially if I were struck with any sudden effort or worry, I used to crap or wet myself. It is something that has taken a very long time to control, through constant practice, but I never saw the need to keep quiet about it. Sometimes I think I rather enjoyed shocking people by telling them. It tended to stop them being patronizing.

Practice helps matters, of course, but the incontinence could still cause difficulties today if, say, I were going to an important meeting. There's nothing worse than spending hours getting laboriously into a suit, then being stuck in a traffic jam and feeling those telltale signs down below. I'd dash off to try and find a loo, but by then it could be too

late, and I'd have to rush off home again to clean myself
up, eventually turning up at the meeting late and in a flus
ter. You have to keep saying to yourself, 'To hell with it,
am not embarrassed. Why should I be? I've got a physica
disability due to having been shot in the Falklands.'

But it does take some time to come to terms with
all that time I have to spend in motorway service station
cubicles, trying to clean myself up.

I believe Beatrice is getting married soon, to someone
in the City. Good old Pathfinder Lawrence, I thought when
I heard, departing again to make way for someone else
That was all a part of the tragedy, looking back. The sor
of thing I seemed always destined to do.

John Lawrence

Like his brothers, Nick had many friends and one o
them had an interest in vintage cars. He had heard o
an H-registration Aston Martin DB6, the original 'James
Bond' car, the owner of which was going abroad and
wanted a quick sale. Nick was round to see it like a shot
having picked up Robert on the way. In two days the dea
was clinched, including the hiring of a lock-up garage in the
flats near us. Robert would be quite prepared to drive over
in the Golf and leave it at our house every time he wanted
to use the Aston. When I asked if it was all a good idea
financially, I was told it was quite definitely an investment.
Cars for me are a means of getting from one place to
another and they are written off at a flat twenty-five per
cent per year. I had difficulty in understanding how any car
could possibly appreciate in value, but I did not argue.

When he brought the car round to show us, almost inevitably there was a new blonde in the front seat. Christina
— Tina for short — was very pretty, with short fair hair
and fascinating pale blue eyes. She had travelled the world
and was a brilliant photographer behind the camera and a
pretty good model in front of it. Now she was working in

he management of pop stars and musicians, something I
new little about.

I marvelled as I looked at the long sleek bonnet of the
ar. It gleamed as Robert gave it yet another rub with his
luster. Once again he was proud to own a car that was just
a little different, one that was definitely special. Quietly I
ave thanks for the new girlfriend as well and thought to
nyself, two down and one (his career) to go.

TUMBLEDOWN

Robert Lawrence

While I was working for Richard O'Brien on *Top People*
I was approached by a journalist called Seamus Milne, who
seemed very interested in my story. He was Thelma Holt's
nephew, and eventually wrote an article, which appeared
in the *Guardian*, outlining what had happened to me
since I was shot in the Falklands War. The feature was
headlined 'Falklands victim the Army tried to forget'. My
neurological surgeon at the Maudsley was furious about
it and told me angrily that he didn't like the image I'd
given of the hospital at all. I felt I had put my views and
described the incidents I'd experienced since the Falklands
quite honestly in the feature, but all in all it caused quite
a stir.

I had a feeling that the Army wouldn't like it either; by
now I was beginning to realize that they didn't approve
of young men like me finding themselves a platform and
speaking out. It broke the spell.

Actress Jane Howe, the leading lady in *Top People*,
was among those who read the article about me in the
Guardian, and she approached me one day about taking
the subject further.

'Look,' she explained, 'my husband has got a great
friend who would be fascinated by this. Can we show him
the piece?'

I said yes of course, and that great friend turned out to
be the writer Charles Wood, whose past work has included
scripting films such as *The Knack, Help!* for the Beatles
and *The Charge of the Light Brigade*. He knew the
film industry extremely well.

'Listen, Robert,' he said, holding up the *Guardian* feature, 'I think we have a great basis here for a screenplay. And what better way could there be for you to get into the film industry, and learn about the business, than to get involved in it?'

Every day after that, actor Mark Burns — Jane Howe's husband — would pick me up from home in London early in the morning and we'd slog down to Banbury to visit Charles. Then I would disappear up to Charles's study and talk with him for hours on end, days on end, weeks on end, until Charles felt he had enough material to write a script. And that script was for a film called *Tumbledown*.

The problem then arose of actually getting the film made, for although Mark and Charles between them had experience of acting and writing, they didn't have the expertise to get a film produced. What we needed was a line producer, a nuts-and-bolts man who knew how to put a film together. We took it to Richard Lester and to David Puttnam, both of whom expressed great interest in it. However, both of them were interested only in making it in their own way, a way that we suspected would have made my own involvement with the production pretty minimal. Charles also saw the project very much as his first opportunity to make the film *he* wanted to make, without the fear of its being adapted later into something he hadn't originally envisaged.

In the end, we came across Alan Wright, who had produced *Wagner*, which Charles Wood had written and for which, coincidentally, I had done the military voice-overs. Alan was young and enthusiastic and seemed determined to help me get the whole project off the ground. While doing so he let me come along with him to work on various other programmes he was making at the time, so that I could gain some experience. One of these was a pilot for a Spike Milligan show called *Last Laugh Before TV AM*. On the day we were due to shoot it, however, Spike rang up to say he wasn't feeling too well, and would it matter if he didn't turn up?

Considering it was a Spike Milligan show, it did matte
rather desperately.

In the end a somewhat panicked Alan Wright got on th
phone to me and said, 'For God's sake, Robert, *you* tall
to him.'

I had spoken to Spike only a couple of times on th
phone before then, but he had had a hard time himself i
the last war — a lot harder than most people realize —
and I sensed he felt a certain empathy with me because o
my own experiences.

'Hi, Robert,' he said, when I called him. 'I'm afraid I'n
not feeling very well.'

'Well, actually, Spike,' I replied, 'to tell you the truth
nor am I. But we've just got to get out there and do i
haven't we?'

It seemed to hit the right note, and eventually I wo
him round and he turned up to do the show.

By then I had learned a great deal about the nuts an
bolts of producing, but the prospect of getting *Tumble
down* made still seemed a long way off. Charles Woo
actually wrote the script for it in late 1984, but it wa
to take years to get what I came to see as this vital an
all-important mission off the ground; years when I woul
often be thrown into the deepest despair, fearing tha
the project that could well change my life would neve
happen.

John Lawrence

Before writing the film script of *Tumbledown*, Charle
Wood also asked to see me and Jean. He came to Londo
with Jane Howe's husband, Mark Burns, and talked — o
rather listened — to me for about three hours. Jea
then joined us for lunch and they talked with her fo
another two.

I wondered what line Charles would take in the script
I knew of his earlier film scripts, and Robert had told m

hat he was very interested in militaria. It seemed to me, therefore, that he was probably a reasonable man who would offer a sympathetic treatment of a complicated and emotive drama.

When I met him I immediately warmed to him, though I have to confess it helped that he was a very good listener. He struck me as an emotional man quite capable of strong feelings, even anger, but essentially a gentle man. Although a professed pacifist in one sense, he had served for six years in the Army and his interest in militaria gave him an insight into war and fighting that was at least founded on practical experience. I got the impression that he was also a man who had probably known tragedy and in consequence had a capacity for understanding and sympathy.

He wrote the script of *Tumbledown* very quickly indeed, and when Robert brought it for me to read I could not put it down until I had finished it.

Understanding a film script is difficult on first reading, so I read it again almost immediately. Then every time I switched on the television I tried to imagine everything I saw and heard on the screen reduced to a script. When I read *Tumbledown* for the third time, my imagination ran riot and I was very moved. It became clear to me that the final interpretation on screen could vary greatly and would depend very much on the director and actors involved. I also came to realize that it was a play about Robert as seen by the author and no one else. One thing it was not was a documentary.

Robert liked the play, but more than that he saw it as a vehicle to take him into the film production world. He and Mark and Charles, largely at Robert's instigation, formed a film production company, LBW Films — the name deriving from the initials of their surnames rather than from any interest in cricket — through which they resolved to make the film as a full-length feature.

Intent on continuing to learn about film production, and with the making of *Tumbledown* remaining a priority, Robert was then befriended by a television film producer who had his own company. Once again Robert could work with him to learn the business, but for no pay. In the old days an apprentice sometimes paid his master and Robert saw this opportunity very much in that light. Production for television was another angle of the business that he needed to know about and, as well as learning, he would widen his circle of friends and contacts still further.

After a few months with this company it seemed like a good idea to involve them in the making of *Tumbledown* and they agreed to make a short video for use in trying to sell it to the American market. Robert had done much of the legwork in LBW's attempts to raise money to back the making of the film and incredibly they had promises of over three million pounds, but all subject to an American distribution deal.

Mark was a professional actor and ideal in looks and voice to be the narrator in the video. They used a few news-clips from the Falklands War, filmed the sentries outside St James's Palace and used several minutes of an interview with Robert sitting on a park bench in his best suit and Guards tie. The final version was quite good although 'over the top' was Robert's description of the script.

The Army public relations people wanted to see it and so did the Scots Guards. They were not impressed either by the video or by the film script and later told Robert he was being manipulated by two charlatans. I had some sympathy with their view of the video but not with their view of the script or of those with whom Robert was working. It was about as accurate as the rumours that later surfaced in the regiment that he had lost all his money and had been heavily involved in drugs.

This lack of understanding and ready acceptance of any suggestion that he had gone off the rails was very hurtful. Robert is intensely proud of his regiment and would never allow any slight or slur upon its name or history to appear in any film or publication with which he had any connection. Unfortunately, it seemed to me that that pride was reciprocated by the regiment only if Robert toed the line and behaved in a totally conventional way. I accept that films that depict any aspect of the regiment have to be totally accurate, but this should not mean that they are therefore acceptable only in documentary form.

Fortunately, Robert, although hurt, was not put off by this attitude and he resolved to press on with trying to market *Tumbledown*. He had come to know, through the Theatre of Comedy, Richard O'Brien of *Rocky Horror Show* fame, and Richard invited him to go to the United States with him for an anniversary production of the show. Robert accepted and used the opportunity to show the *Tumbledown* video to all the big American film distribution companies.

While in the USA two acts of violence upset him. First, his hotel room was broken into while he was asleep and his credit cards were stolen. Secondly, he was taken forcibly down an alley in Greenwich Village and robbed of his wallet at gunpoint. He went wild, shouting at the two young robbers, who fled out of the alley with Robert hobbling in pursuit across the busy street through all the traffic and pedestrians. At the far pavement they dropped the wallet, having removed a fifty-pound note and about a hundred dollars. A taxi driver stopped to help, picked up the wallet, returned it to Robert and took him back to his hotel free of charge.

During the next three weeks Robert received a number of expectant and encouraging telephone calls and each time he phoned me to pass on the excitement. But first one company and then another decided at the last hurdle that there was no market for *Tumbledown* in the United States 'at this moment in time'.

'If they mean now, why don't they say now,' said Robert angrily. As always it was difficult to know just what to say in the face of another disappointment.

Robert Lawrence

I felt great despair at this stage, despair that I had by then spent two years on *Tumbledown* and still had nothing positive to show for it. I had learned a lot during those two years, but felt that no one would ever appreciate how much I had learned unless there was an end product to prove it.

Soon after the American disappointment, Charles Wood's agent came to see me to say that he had had some initial meetings with people at the BBC, and that they might be interested in making the film. But by then I just felt totally exhausted; I felt in volunteering to take on the new and difficult battle presented by this film I had been trying to give myself a reason for living. And after fighting so long and not getting anywhere either with it or with my career, I got into a situation where I couldn't be bothered to try any more.

I entered a deep depression, and became quite ill, and in the end it was decided that I should go on holiday with Tina, with whom I had been going out since the beginning of 1985, to try and cure the general relapse.

We went to the Seychelles, and at the start of the first week I seemed to blow a fuse. I drank a lot and was generally very difficult and tearful. I got upset about not being able to swim properly like everyone else and not being able to walk down to the beach in bare feet like everyone else, and owing to the lack of proper blood circulation, my left-hand side got very badly burned, while my other side went brown. All these little things tallied up into one big depression of frustration and anxiety.

In the second week, as the pressure began to ease and as had often happened in the past, I found myself greatly enjoying my new life, especially with Tina. At times, it was all very difficult for Tina, but she handled the situation very well. People might say that I've been lucky to have met a number of tolerant women; that I've been very lucky with the girlfriends I've had. But then, I've had to learn to be a bit more understanding myself. I spent plenty of time lying in hospital analysing the subject of understanding; how I could get across the degree of understanding I would be needing in the future, and how I would have to be understanding in return. All those times when people used to imply that I was over-reacting, I'd think, sod it, I'm *not* over-reacting, because what matters most in this world is how human beings treat one another. Surely there is nothing more important, and more worth over-reacting to, than the way in which humans treat other humans.

In my heart of hearts, I was hoping to come back from the Seychelles to discover a contract from the BBC and a confirmation that the *Tumbledown* film would be getting under way. But of course, no such thing happened. Nothing new had developed while I'd been away — apart from the fact that the film, as yet unmade, was beginning to attract all sorts of ridiculous political labelling. People reasoned that it would have to be a political film simply because it was about the Falklands War, when in reality it was simply about soldiers and young men; the reasons why young men join armies and want to go to war, and the reality of the possible consequences of their ambitions. I intended it to be an honest and balanced account of what could happen to soldiers, viewed with the benefit of my experiences. But the political fuss went on.

Early on in the development of *Tumbledown* I decided to take a copy of the script to the Ministry of Defence. I wanted them to have their say as soon as possible and, perhaps naïvely, hoped that they might give me some help. Even though I had visions that they might possibly not like the film, I hoped that if I was honest with them, they might be honest with me, and that they could attempt to work with us. Representing fellow soldiers, I thought they'd want people to know what we'd been through in the Falklands, and that they would want society to understand the kind of special attention the victims of such conflicts require.

But I was totally wrong. They didn't want to know. All the publicity that had begun to surround the film was, in their eyes, all rather sordid and unpleasant, and they would really rather I just shut up and keep quiet.

Similarly, the Scots Guards said that they did not like the tone of the film; I think they felt that the coverage of my recovery, particularly, constituted a betrayal, even if I knew it to be the truth.

On the very rare occasions when I bumped into other Scots Guards after I left the Army, rumours would come back to me that they believed I had lost all the money donated to me by the South Atlantic Fund through carelessness and that I had also got seriously into heavy drugs. God knows how such myths originated, but maybe it was all tied in with the sort of image they had of the media industry, and the fear they had of the kind of publicity it could generate. In the late 1980s, the Guards are still desperately trying to cling to their original and traditional way of life and they didn't take kindly to anyone rocking the boat.

When it finally seemed a reality that the BBC would make *Tumbledown*, I received a telephone call one day from the Regimental Adjutant of the Scots Guards.

'Tell me,' he said, 'what's happening about this film?'

So I tried to explain, as I had done before, about the film's major issues, and the beliefs and realities that lay behind it.

When I'd finished, he said, 'Listen, Robert, this is just a gypsy's warning. Stop it.'

The Scots Guards didn't often communicate with me any more. But the film went on.

John Lawrence

The disappointment of not selling *Tumbledown* as a full-length feature film had faded into the background, but the dream of seeing it made somehow, somewhere, sometime was still there. Charles Wood seemed confident that it would eventually be made.

In the meantime, Robert continued to try and get more work in the film industry. He heard that Cannon Films were thinking of making a film about the Falklands War. It would be a typical 'blood and guts' war film that did not ask too many questions — in other words, quite different from *Tumbledown*. Robert wrote to them and secured an interview with the probable producer. At the same time he wrote to the producer of a new film called *White Mischief* which was to be shot mainly in Kenya, a country in which Robert had served. The reply was encouraging in one sense and quite pleasant, but the special advisory requirements had already been met. There might, however, be just a possibility of finding room for Robert on the production team. Much the same applied in the case of a new film about Vietnam. There were, after all, thousands of Vietnam war veterans capable of advising on a film about it. Robert tried to explain that he did not want to be a military adviser, he wanted actually to work in the production. He wrote to the famous film producer Ken Russell, who was also about to start work on a new film. When the reply came, handwritten and on one line, it simply said

Dear Mr Lawrence,

There is no way you could be of any use to me. . . .
                    Yours sincerely,

                    Ken Russell.

When I saw it I was upset. Robert laughed, framed it and hung it on the wall above his desk, confident that the day would come when he could send it back with an appropriate message to make Russell eat his words.

Meanwhile Charles Wood's agent rang one day to say that BBC1 Television had bought the script of *Tumbledown*. Charles said he would be giving Robert one-third of the fee. That was very generous, but only part of the reason for celebration. *Tumbledown* was going to be made: the last skittle was about to go down. First the car, then the girlfriend, and now the film.

Production would start almost immediately, with filming in January 1987. There was already talk of casting and the excitement steadily rose.

Cannon Films decided they were going ahead with their film as well and they definitely wanted Robert to work on it. Why is it that after ages of drought, flood so often follows?

Robert accepted Cannon's offer guardedly and spent a couple of weeks looking at a draft script. He made a number of observations which they accepted and incorporated in a new draft. Once again he went through it, making various suggestions in order to improve the accuracy from a military point of view. He also made suggestions about the individual characters, which greatly enhanced the story-line.

Inevitably it was all too good to be true. First there looked as though there would be a clash between filming dates. The BBC were talking of filming in either the Falklands or the Hebrides, and Cannon in New Zealand. In no way could Robert possibly be in both. Then there were reports of financial problems which might cause Cannon to cancel. Finally a major political row broke over another BBC film about the Falklands written by the dramatist Ian Curteiss.

Curteiss claimed through the press to have been commissioned by Alasdair Milne, Director-General of the BBC, to write the play. This he had done and the BBC had bought the script, but when it reached those whose job it was to produce the drama, he claimed he was asked to rewrite certain parts to show the Prime Minister and the Government in a less good light, she to be uncaring and lacking in compassion, the Government to be interested only in political victory at the next election.

At first the BBC's response to these accusations was muted and weak, suggesting that there had been a huge misunderstanding. Letters in the press from members of the public took sides depending largely on the political colour of the writer. The author himself re-entered the lists and for the first time mentioned *Tumbledown*, saying it was left-wing and therefore politically acceptable to the BBC whereas his own play was not. Charles Wood and I both had letters published pointing out that he had no basis for saying this having never read the script. Charles had something of a reputation for expressing anti-war views and Ian Curteiss had seized on this, but it gave him no grounds to make assumptions in public. Nevertheless, seeds of doubt were sown and I reread the script of *Tumbledown* to make sure I was not being associated with something that was alien to my own beliefs.

Half-way through I began to ask myself what those beliefs were. My twenty-eight years in the Royal Air Force had been unswerving in loyalty to the Crown and unquestioning in terms of political aim, but I began to wonder how much had been instilled in me by my being the child of a serviceman and by the training I had received throughout my career. The role of the armed forces was to keep the peace by deterrent or restore it by swift retribution against an aggressor. It was all quite simple and should not be clouded by such issues as the horrors of war. Of course people were killed in war, it was inevitable, and of course people were maimed in fighting.

I thought of Robert and of his first words he had said to me on his return. Lying in that hospital bed at Wroughton, his head shaved, bits of brain material protruding from

that ghastly black scar, he had said, 'It wasn't worth it
Daddy.'

He had not meant it as at first it sounded. His concern
had been solely that he thought he had been guilty of losing
all his men — but the words have haunted me ever since.

A doctor friend who was a piper had written a number
of tunes, and one he had dedicated to Robert, calling it in
the manner of pipe tunes, 'Lieutenant Robert Lawrence
MC, Scots Guards'. Prompted by him and several others I
had turned the tune into a song called 'South of the Sun',
a reference to the Falkland Islands' being at the extreme
south of the southern hemisphere, not to say the world.
The last two verses ran through my mind as I struggled
with my doubts.

> But the tragedy of battle is so hard to understand
> And the honour and a medal doesn't give me back my
>   hand
> But I'd fight again for freedom 'gainst the tyrant's
>   bloody band
> Be it someone else's islands or my own bonnie land.
>
> Yet the world must not forget us, it must never be
>   in vain
> All the parting and the sorrow, all the bloodshed and
>   the pain
> And though peace on earth, goodwill to men, must
>   always be our aim
> If the need arise for freedom, we would do it all again.

Freedom. Was that the answer perhaps? If so, why was
Robert not free to lead his life as he wished without
having his car vandalized, without being spat upon or
mugged, without some selfish political interest interfering
with almost the first opportunity he had had of working
for a wage since he had been shot?

The filming of *Tumbledown* was put back to September 1987 and as far as Robert was concerned the whole

project was once again in the balance. He became really depressed. He had sometimes been low in spirits, but never as bad as this.

In the summer he had sold the flat in Clapham and had bought a delightful, almost idyllic, cottage in Oxfordshire. It had been built in 1705, had two huge inglenook fireplaces in the living rooms, two bedrooms on the first floor, one of which had been divided by a partition, and two more bedrooms and a shower room in the roof. His first ritual had been to tear down the partition wall on the first floor, exposing another timber beam and making a superb main bedroom. He put a cloakroom in the walk-in sunken pantry and did a lot of redecoration, and within a few weeks had transformed the whole cottage.

The cottage is on the edge of quite a large village, which has an excellent general store, baker, butcher, garage, church and five pubs. It even has its own brewery. For the first few months Robert and Tina were very happy there and although she came to London for her job during the week, Robert often stayed there all the time. We wondered if the comparative isolation was what had brought on the depression, but he insisted it had nothing to do with it. However, I did manage to persuade him to go to the doctor and ask for help, including psychiatric counselling if that was what was needed. After an hour's consultation the doctor suggested he come back in three days' time for a longer appointment. If he needed or felt he wanted additional specialist counselling, then it could be arranged. Robert went back in three days and as far as I could tell talked his way, with the doctor's help, right through and out of the other side of the depression. It had lasted just over six weeks and during that time he had hit rock bottom, but now it seemed he was bouncing back yet again.

Robert decided that he needed a break, preferably in some sunshine, and a week later took off for Cairo. He had no visa before he left, but talked his way through getting one at Cairo airport with the help of a rich Lebanese he had met on the aeroplane. One of the hotel managers also befriended him and he spent four days in his huge country house on the edge of the desert in a village 130 kilometres from Cairo. Desert Arabs joined them one evening and they sat on the verandah talking, smoking their hookahs and drinking thick, sweet Egyptian tea until the early hours. He saw the pyramids and the Sphinx, and in the hotel he met a mercenary out of Nicaragua and three Americans he swore were secret agents. After ten days he came back to London refreshed and ready for anything — except cold.

The cold weather always causes Robert considerable problems. His left arm and hand contract and his left leg lets him down. The incontinence returns, not often, but unpredictably. To begin with Tina had problems coping with that, but she soon got over them.

He began to talk of going abroad permanently. It was not just a question of the grass being greener. Warm weather and a cheaper cost of living were very attractive and he produced advanced ideas of running holiday homes in beach or safari environments on a commercial basis which were very plausible. He wrote to the tourist authorities in some thirty different countries from Cape Verde to Kenya, from the Gulf to Australia, seeking information about currency, population, food and health. I dreaded the thought of his going abroad for good, especially to an area that was in any way unstable, either economically or politically. His mother, however, surprised me by backing him to the hilt. I subdued my feelings and backed him too. After all, it was his life to lead, not mine. Besides, *Tumbledown* was not yet cancelled and filming in September 1987 was still on the stocks so he would not be able to go abroad for a year in any case, and that is a long, long time.

When Remembrance Sunday came round again I asked Robert if he would like to come to the service at St Mary's as he had done the previous year. His mother would be laying the wreath and I would be saying the intercession.

It did not surprise me when he declined. He had found it very harrowing the previous year. Then he amazed me by saying that he and Tina would be going to the service in his village. He would wear his medals; he thought it would be rather nice to take part in something like that in the village where he now lived. Marvellous, but how did it tie up with his hankering to go abroad?

The next time we were in church I looked back to November 1985 when Robert had signed the hand-bound Visitors' Book. In the remarks column he had written a quotation from Brecht:

Do not rejoice in defeat, you men,
For though you put the Bastard down,
The Bitch that bore him is on heat again.

It had shocked me when I first read it and ever since I had tried to interpret it more kindly than it was probably meant. The church had been rebuilt in 1981 to a most beautiful design after being burned down by a crazy arsonist seven years before. The quotation seemed to suggest regeneration, of war maybe, but what is a bitch on heat other than a potential mother hoping to reproduce? In a sense Robert had been regenerated. Certainly he had been snatched from death to live again.

When I got home I looked up Brecht in the *Book of Quotations*. Robert's little gem was not there, but instead I found:

Unhappy the land that has no heroes.
No, unhappy the land that needs them.

I shut the book in dismay and total confusion and tried to restore my equilibrium by remembering what was inscribed in gold letters on the first page of the church Visitors' Book. We had had the book made by a superb craftsman in Lancashire. The cover was blue leather with tooled gold lettering, and in the four corners of each hand-bound page was a stylized thistle design. On the dark-blue watered flysheet in the same gold lettering was written:

> Presented to the Parish Church of St Mary, Barnes
> by the parents of Lieutenant
> ROBERT ALASDAIR DAVIDSON LAWRENCE
> M.C., Scots Guards
> who was severely wounded in the Battle
> of Tumbledown Mountain in the Falklands Campaign 1982.
> It is given in gratitude for his miraculous
> survival, brought about by the Mercy of God, his own
> strength and courage and the Prayers of many,
> including this Congregation.

I felt better and prayed silently, though not as I had done for the previous five years. Now I really felt that I could modify my prayer and say, 'Thank you, God, for giving him strength and courage and hope — and cheerfulness.'

NEW HORIZONS

John Lawrence

The week before Christmas 1986, Charles Wood and Robert were called to the BBC for a meeting with Michael Grade, the Director of Programmes, which had been arranged by Richard Broke, the producer of *Tumbledown*. We guessed this would be make or break for *Tumbledown* and we were very excited, but apprehensive. I did wonder fleetingly to myself just why Robert was going and he must have sensed this because he made it very clear indeed that although the screenplay had been written by Charles, and brilliantly so, the story was quite positively his. Not only that, but for three years he, Robert, had worked to get the film made. At one stage Charles had actually written to say that he wished to withdraw the script, but Robert had rejected this as pure histrionics and had persisted with renewed efforts to get it made. On their arrival at the BBC, Michael Grade was not available because yet another political row had blown up and he was in an emergency meeting. Charles and Robert went to see Richard Broke and he in turn introduced them to Peter Goodchild, Head of Plays. Goodchild had come under a lot of criticism over the Curteiss Falklands play, much of which seemed to me to have been unfair.

The four of them talked for a long time and Robert had to leave the room for a while. Richard Broke, himself confined to a wheelchair, knew Robert quite well, but Peter Goodchild had not met him before. While he was out of the room, so Charles told me later, Goodchild expressed complete amazement and admiration for him and said how delighted he was that Richard intended to

175

use him not only on the production of *Tumbledown* but on its promotion.

After an hour Michael Grade was free and they all went to see him. His first question was, 'Why should we make this film?' After half an hour, his last words before he left were, 'Bring me the finished film of *Tumbledown*.'

Robert telephoned us with the news and we opened a bottle of bubbly, not the best champagne of course; we would save that for the night *Tumbledown* was shown.

* * *

Christmas has always been an important family time for us. Even when they had grown up all three boys were expected, and in general were pleased, to eat with us at home in one gathering on at least one of the three days. When the eldest two were married, the gathering naturally became enhanced by the presence of our daughters-in-law and of course it could now take place in one of their homes instead of ours. For the last two years that pleasure has been further increased by our having become grandparents. I was a little surprised, therefore, at how well Jean accepted Robert's announcement that he would not be with us on Christmas Day because he and Tina wanted to spend Christmas together in the cottage. He hoped, however, that when his brothers had departed from us on Boxing Day with their families to their respective parents-in-law, Jean and I and my aged widowed mother would go down to the cottage for the weekend.

It seemed to be a good arrangement and with appropriate telephone calls and suitable refreshment, Christmas Day passed happily even without his being with us. Roads were quiet on Boxing Day and we all reached our destinations safely.

Robert and Tina seemed very happy and relaxed and we were very happy for them. However, after the first day I

realized that I had not been with Robert for more than a
few hours at a time for years, and seeing the extent of his
ever-present disablement hit me hard.

Tina has a little Pomeranian, a total apology for a
dog in appearance, but an absolute delight in character
and great fun. Robert let it out on to the lawn and it
chased about, leaping in the air and barking, urging him
to play. He accepted the challenge and climbed the patio
steps stiffly, one at a time, holding out his good right hand
as though to catch the animal. The little dog easily avoided
it of course and circled round him excitedly and noisily. As
I watched them playing on the lawn, my eyes filled with
tears. Robert's leg hampered him badly and he could not
turn quickly. His left arm, after swinging uselessly to start
with, began to bend up and his fingers to close with the
exertion. I had to turn away and Jean quietly squeezed
my hand.

Tina did not seem affected in any way and I tried hard
to hide my distress from her. Then I remembered that she
had never known him to be any different and I rejoiced
that she should love him as he was.

In the New Year the cold weather returned and Robert
suffered badly from it. Once again thoughts of emigrating
returned and I was relieved when he began talking of
Australia. It was the other side of the world, but it was
English-speaking, just, and its society similar to Britain's.
Moreover, we had lived there for two and a half years of
the first three of Robert's life.

I recalled those days and pictured him hauling himself
up on the water stand-pipe which was in the middle of
the garden, to stand for the first time. He caught the
drips from the tap in his tiny hand and turned unsteadily
to greet us with a grin widened by his wet fingers stuffed
in his little mouth. I also remembered finding him when
he had crawled for the first time, leaving the rug that
had been spread for him on the lawn. We had been
away only for a moment, but when we returned he
was lifting a stone in the flower bed to reveal a nest

of red-backed spiders. Although not normally lethal, they could give a nasty bite and could make even an adult quite ill.

He laughed when I recounted these memories and mockingly he promised his mother he would not play with the red-backs now he had grown up.

Through cricket I had met the Australian High Commissioner a number of times and so, at Robert's request, I wrote to him to ask if someone on his staff would advise him about emigration. The High Commissioner had gone home at the end of his tour of duty just three weeks before and the new one had not yet arrived, but the acting High Commissioner replied to my letter very kindly, inviting Robert to go and see the Head of Migration at Australia House. He went, was warmly welcomed and received excellent advice.

Robert had been friends for some time with a young Australian living in London who worked for the Australian Broadcasting Corporation, and as the fifth anniversary of the Falklands War drew near, he asked Robert if he could use him as the subject of a short documentary. It seemed like a good idea, providing Robert could determine the broad nature of the material to be used and could have reasonable editorial control. He did not, for instance, want to say something on film that was balanced by a further statement that was then edited out of the final product, leaving only half of the argument. The other possible problem was any restriction placed on his participation by the BBC.

A draft contract had been received by Charles's agent who by then was acting for Robert also, and it had a clause about his not talking to anyone about his story for two years except with BBC permission. He had rejected that, suggested one year only and, on my advice, confirmed by the agent, had insisted that the BBC permission 'should not be unreasonably withheld'.

Since nothing more had been heard and no contract signed, Robert accepted the ABC offer and for two whole days he worked with a camera crew in and around his Oxfordshire cottage.

The fifty-five minutes of unedited video film which resulted was fascinating. When he showed us the finished product I was very impressed by its professional quality and balance, but most of all by the impact it made. Three weeks later we heard from friends in Sydney that they had seen it on Australian television and had been very moved. It transpired that Robert had virtually edited the film himself. I had to admit that, precarious as it might be, Robert was well suited to a career in films or television production.

Just before Easter he announced that he was due a tax rebate and he was therefore taking Tina to Australia for a fortnight's holiday. He had met a number of people through the ABC connection and had been given a list of others to contact in the film and television world in both Sydney and Brisbane. It took him just a week to organize the trip and after a bumpy twenty-two-hour flight they arrived in Sydney. The girlfriend of the ABC producer had offered to put them up and we were able to telephone them there.

Before leaving London, Robert had met a lady called Ainslie Gotto who had been in the public eye some fifteen years before when she had worked for the Australian Prime Minister. By pure coincidence I had served in Egypt with her father thirty years before, when he had been in the Royal Australian Air Force. Together we had produced two plays and two Christmas revues in the fifteen months before I was posted to Aden. I had never seen or heard from him since until Ainslie hit the headlines. She returned to Brisbane two days before Robert and Tina flew to Sydney, and when after a week they moved up to Queensland she made them very welcome and introduced Robert to the head of the Queensland Film Company. Robert came away greatly encouraged.

'It really was very good and the cost of living is definitely cheaper here than at home although houses are not quite as cheap as we had been led to believe.' Robert was talking on the telephone from Brisbane to his mother with great animation and yet seemed more relaxed than he had been for years.

'I haven't definitely made up my mind, but when I asked the Film Company guy if he thought there would be an opening for someone like me out there he said that quite definitely there would be. He told me exactly who to see, but said, "Mind, be sure to come and see me first." '

Jean showed a lot of enthusiasm, and when I got the chance to talk I too tried to make the right noises, convincing myself that the weather and the opportunities for work were what he needed. Twenty-five years before I had coined the phrase 'a land of opportunity because of a dearth of quality'. All those who knew told me this was not true of Australia today. Land of opportunity still, but the quality was so much higher and as for the film industry, that was booming. I had begun to believe it and to share Robert's excitement and expectation.

'This call will be costing a fortune,' I said, thinking it was time to call a halt to the conversation.

'There's one other thing we want to tell you,' he said. 'Tina's going to have a baby.'

I told Jean and we both shouted down the phone with joy. 'Great,' I said. 'Are you going to get married?'

'Yes,' he said, 'as soon as we can, but we've got to tell Tina's parents yet and they're away in America.'

When Robert and Tina got home two days later, we had a good celebration, Jean insisting that we drink the bottle of Dom Perignon given to Robert when he first got back from the Falklands. I opened it carefully and gave him the cork. When I had filled four glasses we all raised them as I offered a simple toast. 'Robert and Tina and your baby, may you have every happiness together and a wonderful life wherever you go and whatever you do.'

Robert grinned and as his grin widened further I no longer saw the slight draw of paralysis in his cheek nor his left arm hanging uselessly by his side.

I turned to Jean and kissed her.

'Aren't we lucky?'

'Yes, very lucky,' she whispered, 'and very blessed too.'

NEW LIFE

John Lawrence

The wedding was perfect in every way. It was a glorious day, Tina looked lovely, Robert proud and smart, and Jean wore a fabulous hat with black and white silk strawberries on it which David Shilling, a friend of Robert's, had made specially for the occasion. Tina's parents, Jim and Joan Rivett, were wonderful hosts and the setting in the old church at Penn was everything one could wish for, with a marvellous reception afterwards at Burnham Beeches. Unusually for such a large gathering, everyone from both sides of the church seemed to mix and share the happiness of the day. Jim, like me, had a big involvement with rugby union football and among the guests were internationals from both Scotland and England, as well as players going back over thirty and forty years from London Scottish, Wasps and Harlequins, who greeted each other like long-lost brothers. Of course there were a lot of young people there too and it was good to see how many friends Robert and Tina had in common. The team of ushers included Mark Mathewson, who had been at Brigade Squad and in the Falklands with Robert, and among the guests were Jeremy Campbell-Lamerton and his wife. Jeremy had also been at Tumbledown, but like Mark had left the Scots Guards now to work in the City. Apart from Robert and his brother, Christopher, they were the only two present from the regiment.

When it was all over, Robert had time to reflect on the previous five years and on the additional responsibility he now had as a husband and which by the end of the year would be increased still further when he became a father.

He sold the Aston Martin, because it was an expensive and impractical car for a family man. His work with the BC on the production of *Tumbledown* was contracted to finish at the end of December and with it, of course, the small additional income that it had brought. His thoughts therefore turned to the future and to what he might do to safeguard it financially. His war disability pension was still assessed as one hundred per cent and as there was clearly no prospect of any physical improvement, hopefully it would remain at that level. Nevertheless it was geared to his being a junior captain and he had no prospect of promotion to major, lieutenant-colonel or even general, as he might have hoped for had he not been shot.

A television programme which Jean and I had seen in October about three soldiers who had been wounded in the Falklands brought to our minds once again the South Atlantic Fund. It had been reported that some fourteen million pounds had been collected through the amazing generosity of the general public and no doubt after suitable investment this had increased to fifteen or even sixteen million pounds. The programme suggested that only some five or six million had been distributed, the three soldiers each having received about one hundred thousand pounds. Such reports are often inaccurate, but even if that figure was in fact only the remaining balance, the impression was clearly given that there was still a significant amount of money to be distributed. I therefore persuaded Robert to write to the Secretary of the Fund enquiring whether there was a possibility of his receiving a further grant to help meet his new responsibilities. The reply he received, dated 30 October, although informative, explained that the Fund was of the nature of an umbrella fund and could not, by its charter, deal directly with applicants. However, they enclosed an application form and an instruction to fill it in and send it via the Scots Guards Charitable Fund, supported by as much additional medical evidence relating to the five years since his discharge as he could possibly obtain. The effect this letter had on Robert was

devastating. His innate abhorrence of hospitals, doctor
and, in particular, forms to be filled in meant that for tw
months he did nothing.

On Sunday, 13 December, Tina gave birth in th
John Radcliffe Hospital in Oxford to a 7 lb 9½ oz bab
boy. On the Thursday they were transferred to the Wa
Memorial Hospital in Chipping Norton. The next day Jea
and I drove down to see our first grandson — albeit ou
fourth grandchild. From our first sight of him he was s
obviously a boy, and naturally the best-looking little bo
there had ever been. I had been in Egypt when Christophe
was born, but I seemed to remember being told the sam
about him and certainly about Nicholas two years later
As for Robert, like his new son he had been born on th
Sabbath day and so, as the saying goes, was bonny and
blithe. For Jean and me, he had just about every othe
virtue as well.

The arrival on the scene of Conrad Alexander Lawrenc
once again brought home the tremendous change i
Robert's circumstances. Over Christmas I persuaded hin
that he should do what the South Atlantic Fund require
and seek to collect as much medical evidence as he coul
relating to his condition throughout the last five years. O
1 January 1988 he wrote what I thought was an excellen
letter to the Secretary of the Fund, with copies sent to th
Scots Guards and his local Member of Parliament.

He began by saying that he was 'steeling myself to
meet the requirements of your office' and went on
to draw an analogy between the Fund and those se
up for the Zeebrugge, Hungerford, King's Cross and
Enniskillen tragedies, and also to highlight the difficultie
of communicating and grasping the feelings of the victims
He then continued:

'I must confess to having loathed my time in hospitals
not always due to my treatment, but I think an under
standable emotion. My one aim was to be discharged an
attempt to resume a normal, or as normal as possible, life
This much I had in common with most patients, military

or otherwise. On discharge I threw myself into building a new life and wherever possible totally avoided any medical or military institution in an attempt to regain my independence. I must say this was an area in which both of the aforementioned institutions helped me greatly. With the exception of being recalled for pension reassessment, something I always felt was looking for my unannounced improvement as opposed to deterioration, I did not see or hear from the Medical or Military world once. There were, however, times when I suffered considerably from both physical and mental pain and on some of these occasions resorted to medical advice. A number of these contacts with both the DHSS and private sector assisted me in some small way, but also transported me back to the frustrating, soul-destroying days of hospitalization.

'After a traumatic breakdown, a period of time at Shrublands Hall, a private health clinic, helped me to come, in some way, to terms with my injury. I decided total avoidance of doctors was the best cure. This decision I stuck with until eventually another particularly black time had me knocking on my new GP's door. He in many ways appeared to care and offer not only medical advice, to be discussed out of surgery, but also the chance to apply for psychiatric help. Unfortunately the very British upbringing of Public School and the Guards saw me solving the problems on my own instead. A military background, especially it seems, makes it difficult to accept help let alone ask for it. That I suppose is my message.

'Like a lot of the injured and bereaved, no doubt, I do not seem to fit the system. I am attempting to track down and write to some of the professionals I have seen, fill in the forms your system produces, and then no doubt have to return to the world of poking, prodding doctors who will reproduce notes that only they can read, and that are already gathering dust in some other filing cabinet anyway.

'Someone else somewhere probably won't have the strength, I'm not sure I have. Dramatic, but true.'

True to his word Robert wrote to Lady de Saumarez at the Shrublands Health Clinic, to Dr Victoria Muir, his GP when he had been living in Sloane Gardens and in Clapham, and to Dr Martin Lawrence, his new GP in Chipping Norton. All wanted to help, although those who had not seen him for a while wanted to update themselves rather than simply say what he had been like when they had last seen him.

The responses from the South Atlantic Fund and the Scots Guards were disappointing to say the least. The Lieutenant Colonel Commanding Scots Guards — whose only other contact had been some six months before, when he had called in first Christopher and then Robert for an interview to suggest that Robert stop the making of *Tumbledown* — wrote to say that he could not understand the contents of the letter. He was nevertheless quite willing to help if that was what Robert required. The Secretary of the South Atlantic Fund did not reply, but it was eventually explained on the telephone to me by the Regimental Adjutant that the Secretary had similarly had difficulty in understanding the letter, not knowing whether it was asking for help or merely making comment. After all, if help was required, an application form had been sent to Robert with the letter of 30 October.

As well as to Shrublands and the other doctors, Robert had written to the Queen Elizabeth Military Hospital, Woolwich. There his letter was seen by a lieutenant-colonel in the Royal Army Medical Corps who seemed to recognize the underlying stress that Robert was experiencing. In consequence he called the hospital and arranged for Robert to be admitted. However, instead of telephoning to check that this would be acceptable to him and, indeed, convenient, they sent him a letter which simply said that arrangements had been made for him to be admitted to Ward 2 on 1 February, just over a week later.

Once again Robert was devastated. There was no way he wished to see that hospital and most especially that particular ward ever again.

He telephoned me to explain how he felt and we discussed the matter at length. Finally, he was persuaded that everyone was trying to help. However, we were not sure at that stage who had initiated the call to Woolwich. Was it just routine to check on his progress? If so, it was the first such call since he had been discharged. Perhaps someone had had a touch of conscience. Maybe the Secretary of the South Atlantic Fund had made the arrangement in order to obtain the medical support needed for a further grant — much better actually to do something than just write a letter. Not that we could really understand why further medical evidence was required. Like others, no doubt, Robert was not going to improve, and if the money had been donated for Falklands victims, wounded or bereaved, then why could it not be distributed in full?

My telephone calls to the Secretary of the Fund and the Regimental Adjutant soon revealed that neither had been responsible for the appointment. However, the Adjutant went to quite a lot of trouble to find out how it had all happened. The intention, apparently, was to assess Robert with two things in mind. First, they would do what they could to support a possible further claim and secondly, they would like to see if anything could be done by way of surgery or treatment to improve his lot physically.

This seemed to put Robert's mind at rest and on the due date he arrived at the Lieutenant-Colonel's office, having first telephoned to say that he would attend for any appointment made for him, but under no circumstances would he agree to being admitted.

When we saw him that evening it was obvious that he had had a very harrowing day. Jean and I were both upset by his distress, but I felt it would be better to talk it out of him if at all possible and so, after phoning Tina, he told us all about what had happened.

First of all he had been shown into the Lieutenant-Colonel's office. He had seemed very nice, but nice or not, Robert had jumped straight in with both feet, telling him just what he thought of the system. He could not believe the response it had brought from the Colonel. 'You know, Robert, you have a problem. I have seen your letter, I've listened to you now. You are quite right; the system does not work; it has not looked after you; it is not geared to; it cannot afford to. There are only two military hospitals in any way capable of helping you, Woolwich and Aldershot, and they are too busy looking after serving soldiers. The money is not there and basically, yes, you are an embarrassment.'

We could imagine how Robert felt. The Colonel seemed to have confirmed what we had really known ever since he had got home from the Falklands. People just do not want to know.

I suppose to be fair we had to accept that the Colonel appeared to want to help. Indeed, he had said that they would examine Robert thoroughly to see if there was anything that could be done to improve his physical condition, but he had also said that his problem was possibly more in the mind. We were not too happy about that. However, his promise that they would produce a report that he felt would undoubtedly be sufficient to enable to the South Atlantic Fund to make a further grant was encouraging.

Robert was obviously shattered by what the Colonel had said about the system, even though it added weight to the point that I think Robert has tried to make throughout. The point is that in future the Army must be totally honest with those young men who seek to join it. It is all very well telling them that it is a good life, an exciting and challenging life, but they may be called upon to go to war and if so they may get hurt. What the Army must stop telling them is that they will get special consideration afterwards if they are hurt. It is just not true in Robert's view, and the Colonel seemed to be confirming that view.

I believe Robert thoroughly enjoyed being a soldier; in many ways he even enjoyed the battle for Tumbledown Mountain, he enjoyed the challenge — but he now seemed totally disillusioned by the attitude shown towards him.

To be told that he had to go through yet another bout of medical examinations and would have to spend ages filling in yet another form was very disappointing. It all seemed so unnecessary. He was not going to get any better. The DHSS reassess him for his pension very year. Why on earth could copies of that assessment not be supplied to the Army, and the South Atlantic Fund, and the Scots Guards, or anyone else who needed to see it?

Of course, the Scots Guards have an introvert narrow-mindedness which must make it very difficult to cope with the likes of Robert. They still tend to live in the past. I believe it is true that, according to Household Division Orders, it is not acceptable for an officer to be seen carrying a package in public or using public transport in London — not an unreasonable rule if he is in tunic and bearskin, but in civilian clothes? Such things may be taken with a pinch of salt and in many ways the Scots Guards more than some of the other regiments appreciate the need for regulations to be practicable and modern, but their obsession with the past seems to inhibit them and there appears to be little doubt that Robert is an embarrassment to them.

Robert was close to tears after his interview with the Colonel and we felt for him the utter despair which seemed to come from the fact that what had been so much pride in his regiment had now become so much disappointment and disillusionment — almost as though he had let them down by getting so badly wounded and they therefore had no further use for him.

Some years ago Jean had a wonderful collection of coronation mugs going right back to Queen Victoria, Edward VII, George V, even a full set of cup, saucer, plate and mug for the uncrowned Edward VIII. They used to stand on a radiator shelf in the hall. One day I came into the house to find the telephone ringing. Hurriedly I switched off the burglar alarm, dropped my briefcase, grabbed the phone and slumped down into the chair beside it. The chair slid backwards on the tiled floor and I and it crashed into the shelf. It tipped forwards and every coronation mug, cup, plate, saucer, the lot, fell to the floor.

About four survived; the rest were smashed to smithereens, chipped, cracked or broken in several pieces. I picked out those that I thought could be saved or mended, but when Jean came home she was heartbroken and threw all but the unharmed four into the dustbin. She would not have chipped or cracked pieces among those that were whole, no matter how treasured they had been in her original collection.

I wondered if that was how the Scots Guards felt about Robert. In a way I could understand it if they did but, for all he served Her Majesty, he is no coronation mug.

Eight years before, I had had two sons in the Scots Guards and could not have been more proud. Now, Christopher had insisted on leaving (and they had not liked it at the time) because he had wanted a more lucrative career, and Robert seemed to have lost practically all respect for them. I was totally bewildered and not a little angry that such a fine regiment should have allowed this to happen to two such fine officers.

* * *

It delighted but surprised us that Robert and Tina did not seem to want to live in London any more. They appeared to like living in the country because it has a certain peace about it. Their cottage is beautiful and ideal for them, though Robert talks of probably having to sell it to recoup his financial position.

He had worked extremely hard on many aspects of the production of *Tumbledown*, especially when on location, and with this experience behind him, he hopes to get work in the film industry from time to time. It is a precarious career, but he really enjoys it and undoubtedly has a flair for it. I believe he will do very well in it, given the opportunity.

His main problem is the British weather and I think it quite likely that they will eventually emigrate to Australia where the climate should help to make Robert's life a lot more physically comfortable. Tina has lived there before and seems happy to go, and although she has expressed some concern about leaving the vast network of friends and family from whom they get so much support, I am sure they would soon overcome that difficulty. After all, they already have friends out there, and it would be a great place to bring up Conrad.

It might be difficult if Conrad were ever to want to join the Army, and I do not know what Robert would say to him if he did. But it is a pleasant thought that, having grown up with and got used to a father with virtually only half a body, one day Conrad will learn what his father did and how he came to be as he is.

I believe that deep down Robert still loves the old things, the sort of things that I was brought up to believe in and that I tried to bring him up to believe in. He still loves Kipling and has already bought Conrad *The Jungle Books* (and Charles Wood has given him *Gunga Din*). Robert has also bought him *Kidnapped* and *Robin Hood* and *Children of the New Forest*. When Conrad is old enough to have them read to him and then to read them for himself I hope he enjoys them as much as Robert and I do. And I hope he can learn from them as Robert seems to have done, not only the true values of courage, love, devotion to duty, selflessness, valour and chivalry, but also that these must apply in times of peace as well as war.

Robert Lawrence

I still believe that what I did in the Falklands War was worth doing. I still believe that what I did had to be done. When thousands of fighting troops suddenly march into your house to tell you, with the barrel of a gun stuck up your nose, that you must no longer speak English, but Spanish, you have a right to be defended by any civilized nation.

And I had, and still have, this white-hot pride. The kind of pride that the Army trains young soldiers to build up. The kind of pride that enables them to go off to war and fight and kill for what they are taught to believe in; principles like freedom of choice and of speech.

What I didn't realize, until, like so many others, I came back crippled after doing my bit for my country, was the extent to which we had been conned. Conned into believing in a set of priorities and principles that the rest of the world and British society in general no longer gave two hoots about. We had been 'their boys' fighting in the Falklands, and when the fighting was over, nobody wanted to know.

The indifference, embarrassment, exploitation and countless bureaucratic cock-ups that followed my return home were not what I'd expected. They opened my eyes. They changed me. They changed my father, a great patriot, with twenty-eight years in the RAF behind him. He believed so strongly in the forces, and believed 'the system' would look after us all. I think the reality shook him. It was almost as if a staunch Christian, who had always lived and acted in a respectful Christian way, were suddenly being made to question God.

He was always prepared to throw his weight around on my behalf, and did so after I came home. He knew the forces system, and the language of the system, and the right people he should be contacting to help me at any time. What's frightening is how much I still suffered despite having the sort of father I had, doing all that. It made me wonder, if this was happening to me, an officer with a supportive forces family, what the hell was happening to the injured Guardsman whose father was an out-of-work shipbuilder in Glasgow, or an out-of-work miner in Wales?

People have been told how bloody the First World War was, and how bloody Vietnam was, but they have not been told how bloody the Falklands War was. And I have a duty now, I believe, to inform my generation not only about what the fighting was like, but about what can happen to you if you get injured, in some sort of attempt to make them think twice about getting involved in another war.

The time has now come for me to look to the future. I have found the pawing and raking over of the past difficult and I now want to look forward, but at the same time I want people to understand.

My story, I am sorry to say, has no conclusion. The battles go on and no doubt other people will dig deep into the scandals of the South Atlantic Fund and point out once again the lack of understanding among those who stick to the old rules.

I will, I have no doubt, be accused of being bitter. I am. Not bitter about the war, the injury, or even my disability, but bitter about the pretence of real care and above all bitter about the small-mindedness which stops us changing as a society or race. An attempt at real honesty has left me open to attack, but I believe it is time to be big enough to be honest and admit weaknesses which, after all, are part of human nature.

I intend to live an exciting and adventurous life with Conrad and Tina. I intend to have time for them and to beat the realities of the 1980s Western world. Maybe I'll be lucky enough to succeed.

When I was awarded the Military Cross I had a lot of wonderful letters from all sorts of people. One, from the US Army Attaché, said:

'The courage, valour and professionalism you displayed during the Falkland Islands operation has earned you not only the proper praise of your country, but the esteem of all your military comrades. You have vividly demonstrated that the individual soldier remains the ultimate determinant on the battlefield. Congratulations on the award of your Military Cross from the Officers and men of the United States Army.'

It looks good in my scrapbook among the other letters from dukes and generals and goes with the group photographs of Brigade Squad, Sandhurst rugby team, Right Flank in Belfast and the Jungle Warfare Course that hang in the cloakroom. Over the inglenook fireplace is the regimental badge of the Scots Guards, made for me specially by the Honorary Woodcarver to the Lord Lyon, King of Arms, and the Council of Scottish Clan Chiefs.

If we go to Australia I expect the photographs will come down. I don't think the plaque ever will, though it might get moved to the cloakroom. The rest is in the past and I hope one day everyone I talk to will know about it and I'll not have to talk about it any more.

INDEX